WITHDRAWN

44 KT-523-416

PROGRAMMING

FOR EVERYONE

IN JAVA

Springer
New York
Berlin
Heidelberg
Barcelona
Hong Kong
London
Milan
Paris
Singapore
Tokyo

PROGRAMMING FOR EVERYONE IN JAVA

PER BRINCH HANSEN

Per Brinch Hansen
Syracuse University
Syracuse, NY 13244
USA
pbh@top.cis.syr.edu

UNIVERSITY OF HERTFORDSHIRE
HATFIELD CAMPUS LRC
HATFIELD AL10 9AD 292192

BIB 0387986839

CLASS 005· 133 JAV

LOCATION FWL

BARCODE 4404907707

Library of Congress Cataloging-in-Publication Data
Brinch Hansen, Per, 1938–
        Programming for everyone in Java/Per Brinch Hansen.
            p.   cm.
        Includes bibliographical references and index.
        ISBN 0-387-98683-9 (softcover : alk. paper)
        1. Computer programming I. Title.
    QA76.73.J38B74   1999
    005.13′3—dc21   98-51800

Printed on acid-free paper.

Java is a trademark of Sun Microsystems, Inc. Macintosh is a trademark of Apple Computer, Inc.
Unix is a trademark of X/Open Company, Ltd.

© 1999 Springer-Verlag New York, Inc.
All rights reserved. This work may not be translated or copied in whole or in part without the
written permission of the publisher (Springer-Verlag New York, Inc., 175 Fifth Avenue, New York,
NY 10010, USA), except for brief excerpts in connection with reviews or scholarly analysis. Use
in connection with any form of information storage and retrieval, electronic adaption, computer
software, or by similar or dissimilar methodology now known or hereafter developed is forbidden.
The use of general descriptive names, trade names, trademarks, etc., in this publication, even if
the former are not especially identified, is not to be taken as a sign that such names, as understood
by the Trade Marks and Merchandise Marks Act, may accordingly be use freely by anyone.

The programs in this book are included for their instructional value. They have been tested with
care but are not guaranteed for any particular purpose. The author and publisher of this book
shall not be liable in any event for incidental or consequential damages in connection with, or
arising out of, the furnishing, performance, or use of these programs.

Production managed by MaryAnn Cottone; manufacturing supervised by Joe Quatela.
Camera-ready copy prepared from the author's LaTeX 2$_\varepsilon$ files.
Printed and bound by R.R. Donnelley and Sons, Harrisonburg, VA.
Printed in the United States of America.

9 8 7 6 5 4 3 2 1

ISBN 0-387-98683-9 Springer-Verlag New York Berlin Heidelberg   SPIN 10703480

In memory of
Ole Bak and Ole Riis

PREFACE

THE MAIN GOAL

This is a book about computer programming for beginners. I assume that you know very little or nothing about how computers work and how you program them. I will show you how to write understandable computer programs in *Java*, a programming language that is widely used on the Internet.

Now, why should you be interested in computer programming? After all, most of you will probably not become professional programmers. Well, the most important reason I can think of is simply that computer programming is *fun*. You will enjoy learning a new skill and becoming good at it.

And, in today's world, it is important for professionals in any field to appreciate what computers can (and cannot) do well. To reach this level of understanding, you must go beyond the routine skills of a computer user and learn the art of programming in some depth.

KEY FEATURES

While emphasizing *general principles* of programming, this book

- Uses examples from the *humanities* only, without any mathematics or engineering.

- Explains all programming concepts by means of *complete programs*.

- Concentrates on *exercises* solved by writing complete programs.

- Takes you from *text input/output* to *object-oriented programming* in one semester.

- Gives you a solid *background* for a second course on the graphics and networking facilities of Java.

THE PROGRAMMING LANGUAGE JAVA

This is *not* a book about the programming language Java. I only explain what you need to know about Java to understand the programming examples and solve the exercises.

Although you will be using Java in this course, the same methods can be used for systematic programming in other languages, such as C, Fortran, and Pascal.

It is too early to tell whether Java will become the standard language in introductory courses on computer programming. There are unmistakable symptoms of unnecessary complexity in Java, which are confusing for beginners (and for me as well).

The only features of Java I use are those that simplify the programmer's task. To help you stay clear of the pitfalls of Java, I recommend some restrictions on the use of the language. Brief examples demonstrate violations of these restrictions. Rather than attempting to explain the obscure effects of these examples, I show you how to rewrite them and avoid the pitfalls.

TEACHING AIDS

This first course concentrates on programs for *text processing*. Since standard Java is inconvenient for text input/output, I have written a simple programming interface, called the *Java text program*. This Java program

- Defines identical output methods for screen and disk files, similar to the write procedures of Pascal.

- Defines identical input methods for keyboard and disk files, similar to the read procedures of Pascal.

- Uses single-character lookahead for syntax-directed input.

- Requires a single compilation only.

The Java text program is defined by a text file, named `text.java`. The instructor can obtain this file by anonymous file transfer from the directory `pbh/textprogram` at `ftp.cis.syr.edu` and distribute it to you by E-mail. Appendix A explains how you compile this program in your own directory.

I have used the Java Developer's Kit (JDK) from Sun Microsystems and my own Java text program to program all examples and exercises. And I have tested these Java programs under both Macintosh System 7.5 (JDK 1.0.2) and Unix (JDK 1.1.2).

TEACHING EXPERIENCE

At Syracuse University, I have taught this course to undergraduates in Arts and Sciences, Management, Public Communications, Visual and Performing Arts, Engineering, and Computer Science (see the *Sample Class Schedule* in Appendix B).

I have learned that it is possible to teach students from *any* field of study to write computer programs. But novices must be taught by an experienced programmer. It is *not* a task for a teaching assistant. It is, however, essential to supplement classes with a programming lab run by a teaching assistant, who can help students with language details and problems of compilation and execution.

Acknowledgments

I would like to thank Josh Berdine, Thomas Brinch Hansen, and David Jakel for many detailed helpful comments.

Permission to quote from the following sources is gratefully acknowledged:

Per Brinch Hansen, *Operating System Principles.* Prentice Hall, Englewood Cliffs, NJ, 1973. Copyright © 1973 by Prentice Hall.

Per Brinch Hansen, *The Architecture of Concurrent Programs*, Prentice Hall, Englewood Cliffs, NJ, 1977. Copyright © 1977 by Prentice Hall.

Per Brinch Hansen, *Studies in Computational Science: Parallel Programming Paradigms*, Prentice Hall, Englewood Cliffs, NJ, 1995. Copyright © 1995 by Prentice Hall.

Per Brinch Hansen, Monitors and Concurrent Pascal: A personal history. In T. J. Bergin, Jr. and R. G. Gibson, Jr. Eds. *History of Programming Languages II*, 121–172, ACM Press, New York, 1996. Copyright © 1996 by Association for Computing Machinery, Inc.

Per Brinch Hansen, *The Search for Simplicity: Essays in Parallel Programming.* IEEE Computer Society Press, Los Alamitos, CA, 1996. Copyright © 1996 by The Institute of Electrical and Electronics Engineers, Inc.

Thomas Brinch Hansen, *The Brain*, unpublished poem, 1975. Copyright © 1975 by Thomas Brinch Hansen.

Good Time Crossword Puzzles, Crossword 1, *Good Time Crossword Puzzles, No. 126.* Penny Press, Norwalk, CT, March 1997. Copyright © 1997 by Penny Press.

Gerald Maguire, *Create Your Own Shakespearean Insults*, unpublished list of words, 1988. Copyright © 1988 by Gerald Maguire.

PER BRINCH HANSEN
Syracuse University

CONTENTS

LIST OF PROGRAMS

LIST OF EXERCISES

1

SIMPLE PROGRAMS

To solve a problem on a computer you must write a *program*, that is, a sequence of instructions for the computer to follow. This chapter explains how you write and execute simple programs.

1.1 HOW COMPUTERS WORK

1.1.1 Cooks and Recipes

A *cookbook recipe* is similar to a computer program. Here is my grandmother's recipe for cookies:

PORTUGUESE COOKIES

```
Mix 250 grams of butter and 250 grams of sugar and stir until white;
then add 5 eggs, one at a time. Stir well before adding 250 grams of
flour and a bit of currant. Use a spoon to place the cookies on a
baking sheet and bake them in a well-heated oven.
```

The recipe lists the *ingredients* of the cookies and the *instructions* you must follow to make them. The recipe itself is just a *text*. To make the cookies, you must *follow* the instructions. The recipe does not explain the instructions in complete detail. You need experience and common sense to interpret the meaning of *informal statements*, such as "a bit of currant" and "a well-heated oven."

1.1.2   Computers and Programs

In contrast to a recipe, a computer program must be written in a precisely defined notation that does not depend on human experience and interpretation. This *formal notation* is called a *programming language.*

The invention of programming languages is surely one of the most significant milestones in the history of computing. The science writer, Isaac Asimov (1976), put it this way:

> I strongly suspect that the advance of science or any branch of it depends upon the development of a simple and standardized language into which its concepts can be put. Only in this manner can one scientist understand another in his field.

A programming language is a *practical tool* you can use to solve *specific problems* on a computer. But above all, it is a *standardized notation* that enables programmers to understand *general concepts* of computing. Without such a notation, I could not write this book. The failure to understand this deep insight may explain why so many programmers are content to use *any* programming language, and do not seem to care whether it is *simple* and *precisely defined.*

In theory, a programming language can only serve as a *standard* if it is concisely defined in a *language report.* In practice, however, most language definitions rely heavily on the reader's ability to fill in gaps and remove inconsistencies by educated guessing. I believe there is a reason for this sad state of affairs (Brinch Hansen 1996):

> The task of writing a language report that explains a programming language with complete clarity to its implementors and users may look deceptively easy to someone who hasn't done it before. But in reality it is one of the most difficult intellectual tasks in the field of programming.

The quality of a language report is crucial to professional programmers who write large programs. But, since a language definition is a rather terse document, most beginners prefer to learn a programming language from an informal description (such as this book) and use the official report only to look up the finer details of language features.

We will use the programming language *Java,* defined by Gosling (1996).

The *ingredients* of a program are *data,* known as *input,* which are used by a computer to produce new data, known as *output.* I will only discuss programs, which use text files as input/output. A *text file* is a sequence of characters. It is either an existing text file, input from a disk or a keyboard, or a new text file, output to a disk or a screen.

The *instructions* of a program define a sequence of computer operations, which use input files to produce output files.

Writing a program text is the most creative part of computer programming. The computer is used for the more routine aspects of *program development*:

- First, you *type* the program and save it as a text file. You do this by means of a standard program, called a *text editor*. At this stage, the program is just another *text*. You can edit and print it, but the computer cannot execute it (yet).

- Then, you use another standard program, called a *compiler*, to translate the program text into *program code* that can be executed by the computer.

- Finally, you use a computer to *execute* the program code.

In this book, I will only explain what a computer does when it runs a Java program. In a first course, I cannot explain in greater detail how computer hardware and software work. If you are interested in that, you must take courses in electronics, computer architecture, compilers, and operating systems.

However, there is no reason to do that. Every explanation must stop at some level of detail, where certain things are taken for granted. Otherwise, it takes forever to learn a new subject.

So, I will take a much simpler view of computers: a programming language, like Java, hides the complicated details of a real computer, and lets you think of it as a much simpler *abstract computer*, let's call it the *Java computer*. From your point of view (and mine too), the rules of the Java language define how this computer works.

This is my answer to the question: *how does a computer work?* In this course, *it works like Java!*

1.1.3 Getting Started

To be able to use text files in your Java programs, you must create a new directory for all your Java programs and install a standard program, called the *Java text program*, in this directory (as explained in A.1). Then you are ready for the first Java program!

1.2   THE FIRST PROGRAM

I will illustrate the main phases of program development and show you how to write, type, compile, edit, and run a program.

1.2.1   Text Output

Let's begin with a simple problem: how do you write a program that makes the computer display the line

```
Hello World
```

on the screen?

A program treats the *screen* as a *text file*, which will be output as a sequence of characters. Before the program can use the screen for output, the computer must perform an initial housekeeping operation, called the *opening* of the file.

A program instruction that makes the computer do something is called a *statement.* The first statement opens the screen for output:

```
output out = new output();
```

Notice that the statement ends with a *semicolon.*

In general, a program may use several text files. To distinguish between different files, a program must give each file a different *name*. The open statement, shown above, introduces the name `out` to refer to the screen file. This name is chosen by the programmer.

The next statement instructs the computer to write the line `Hello World` on the screen:

```
out.writeln("Hello World");
```

This output statement has three parts:

- the name of the file `out`,

- the name of an output operation `writeln`, and

- a text string `"Hello World"` enclosed in quotation marks.

Before the program ends, the computer must perform a final housekeeping operation, called the *closing* of the screen file. The following statement closes the screen for further output:

```
out.close();
```

1.2.2 Blocks and Programs

So far I have written three statements that define the effect of the program:

```
{ output out = new output();
  out.writeln("Hello World");
  out.close();
}
```

The statements are enclosed in curly brackets to show that, conceptually, they belong together as a unit. It is called the *main block* of the program.

The program is still not complete. The missing details vary from one programming language to another. In Java, the `main` block must be included in a *program skeleton* of the form:

```
class skeleton extends basic
{ public static void main(String param[]) throws Exception
  /* insert the main block here */
}
```

At this stage, the notational details of the skeleton are not important. We will just accept it as it is.

Two things are needed to turn the skeleton into a complete program: First, the word `skeleton` must be replaced by a program name, say, `hello`, chosen by the programmer. And then the `main` block must be inserted where it belongs in the skeleton:

```
class hello extends basic
{ public static void main(String param[]) throws Exception
  { output out = new output();
    out.writeln("ello World");
    out.close()
  }
}
```

In putting this program together, I have deliberately made two minor mistakes, which are typical of the clerical errors that always creep into even the most carefully written program.

1.2.3 Edit, Compile, and Run

Your first task at the computer is to use a text editor to *type* the program as a text file, named `hello.java`. Please make sure that the file is placed in your *Java directory* (see A.1). And type the program text *exactly as shown above*, even if you recognize my programming mistakes.

Your next task is to *compile* the program text into executable code. On a *Unix* system, you start a compilation by typing the command

```
javac hello.java
```

The compiler will recognize one of the programming errors and display the message:

```
hello.java, Line 5: ';' expected
out.close()
```

The message includes the incorrect line, `out.close()`, and a ˆ mark that shows where the error is on the line. Since the compiler found a programming error, it did not generate code.

You must now *edit* the text file `hello.java` by adding a semicolon at the end of line 5. The program text should then look like this:

```
class hello extends basic
{ public static void main(String param[]) throws Exception
  { output out = new output();
    out.writeln("ello World");
    out.close();
  }
}
```

Then you *recompile* the program by typing the command

```
javac hello.java
```

again. When the compilation is finished and you list your Java directory, you will see that the *program code* is stored in a new file, named `hello.class`.

Now, you are ready to *run* the program to see if it works correctly. When you type the command

```
java hello
```

the computer executes the program code and displays the line

```
ello World
```

on the screen.

Since the letter `H` obviously is missing in the output string, you need to use the editor to correct the program text before compiling and running it again. The two typing mistakes show that the compiler can detect some, but not all, programming errors. You must find the remaining ones by *testing* the program.

1.2.4 The Program "Hello"

The final version of the first program is shown below:

Program 1.1 *Hello World.*

```
class hello extends basic
{ public static void main(String param[]) throws Exception
  { output out = new output();
    out.writeln("Hello World");
    out.close();
  }
}
```

Since the program includes the program name `hello`, it must be stored in a text file, named `hello.java`. When you compile and run this program, the computer executes the statements of the `main` block, one at a time in the order written, and displays the line `Hello World`, on the screen.*

When the computer reaches the end of the program, the execution *terminates*. The operating system is now ready to accept another user command from the keyboard.

1.2.5 Some Terminology

At this point, it is useful to introduce some Java *terminology*:

- A *method* is a named operation, such as `writeln`.

- A *class* is a named group of related methods. The above program uses two methods, `writeln` and `close`, from a class, named `output`. This class is defined by the Java text program.

- The **open** operation, which initializes a new output file, is called a *constructor* (instead of a method).

Earlier, I said that the statement

```
out.close();
```

---

*To compile the same program on a *Macintosh* system, use the mouse to drag the `hello.java` icon and drop it on top of the `Java Compiler` icon. To run the compiled program, drop the `hello.class` icon on top of the `Java Runner` icon.

"closes the screen for further output." Strictly speaking, a statement doesn't *do* anything. It is just a piece of *text* that can be edited, printed, and compiled. It is the *execution* of the compiled statement that closes the file. The statement itself only *denotes* this operation. However, to avoid such cumbersome language, I will often say informally that a statement performs an operation.

Similarly, when I say that a program has a certain effect (or that it terminates), I am not talking about the program text, but about what happens when a computer executes the compiled program.

1.3 INPUT/OUTPUT

Here is an old magic trick: Think of a number, multiply it by 5, add 6, multiply by 4, add 9, and multiply by 5. If you tell me the final result only, I can easily "guess" the original number.

1.3.1 Screen Output

A program that performs this trick uses the *screen* to ask you a series of questions and display the original number. To vary the theme a bit, I will call the screen file `sink` (instead of `out`):

```
{ output sink = new output();
  sink.writeln("Think of a number");
  sink.writeln("Multiply it by 5");
  sink.writeln("Add 6");
  sink.writeln("Multiply by 4");
  sink.writeln("Add 9");
  sink.writeln("Multiply by 5");
  sink.writeln("Type the final result");
  . . .
}
```

The ellipsis points ... are not part of the program. They just show that some details have been omitted.

When this block is executed, the following lines immediately appear on the screen:

```
Think of a number
Multiply it by 5
Add 6
Multiply by 4
Add 9
Multiply by 5
```

```
Type the final result
```

You can now follow these instructions and write down your numbers on a piece of paper, say,

```
I am thinking of 1997
1997 times 5 is 9985
9985 plus 6 is 9991
9991 times 4 is 39964
39964 plus 9 is 39973
39973 times 5 is 199865
```

1.3.2 Keyboard Input

The program asks you all the questions before you have had a chance to even think of a number! To add some magic to the program, it should only ask one question at a time, say

```
Think of a number
```

and *pause* while you write down your answer to that question.

To be able to do that, the program opens the *keyboard* as an input file:

```
input source = new input();
```

The open statement includes the name of a class **input** and the name of the file **source**. The **input** class defines input methods for text files. It is a part of the Java text program. The file name is introduced by me.

The statement

```
source.readln();
```

uses an input method **readln** to make the computer wait until you press the *return* key. This statement is used in the revised block shown below:

```
{ input source = new input();
  output sink = new output();
  sink.writeln("Think of a number");
  source.readln();
  sink.writeln("Multiply it by 5");
  source.readln();
  sink.writeln("Add 6");
  source.readln();
  sink.writeln("Multiply by 4");
  source.readln();
  sink.writeln("Add 9");
  source.readln();
```

```
sink.writeln("Multiply by 5");
source.readln();
sink.writeln("Type the final result");
...
}
```

Each `writeln` statement displays a *different* text string. The string output by a particular statement is called the *actual parameter* of that statement. As an example, the actual parameter of the statement

```
sink.writeln("Think of a number");
```

is the string `"Think of a number"`.

1.3.3   Variables and Assignment

The program needs a place to *record* the final result when you type it, and must be able to *retrieve* it again to compute the original number.

Now, the computer keeps data in an electronic *memory*, which is divided into millions of *memory locations*. Each memory location can hold a single data value, such as an integer or a character.

In a programming language, memory locations are known as *variables* and are described by statements, called *variable declarations.*

The variable declaration

```
int result;
```

introduces a new variable, named `result`. The symbol `int` shows that this variable will be used to hold an integer value (as opposed to, say, a character). We will call it an *integer variable*, or a variable of *type integer*.

When the program is executed, the computer automatically selects an unused memory location for the variable. We will ignore the details of how this is done and just say that the execution of the variable declaration *creates* a new variable by magic.

The use of the variable to record a value is called *variable assignment.* The *assignment statement*

```
result = source.readint();
```

is executed in two steps:

1. The `readint` method inputs an integer from the `source` file (which is the keyboard). You must type the integer on the keyboard, say, `199865`, and press return.

2. This integer is assigned to the variable `result`.

The variable declaration and the assignment statement can be combined into a single statement:

```
int result = source.readint();
```

The advantage of this notation is that it clearly shows that the variable has a well-defined value from the beginning. It is called an *initialized variable*.

1.3.4 Expressions

When the program has input and recorded your final result, it "guesses" your original number in three steps:

```
Take the final result: 199865
Subtract 165:           199700
Divide by 100:            1997
```

If you think of another number, say 23, the final result (2465) will be different. But the above rule still gives the original number (23). Try it!

The program uses an *arithmetic expression*

```
(result - 165)/100
```

to compute the original number. When the variable name `result` is used in an *expression,* it denotes the *value* of the variable. Since the variable has the value 199865, the value of the expression is 1997 by the usual rules of arithmetic.

The output statement

```
sink.writeln((result - 165)/100);
```

is executed in two steps:

1. The expression is evaluated to obtain the integer value 1997.

2. This value is output to the `sink` file (which is the screen).

If you want the program to display a longer message of the form:

```
My guess is that your original number was 1997
```

you may try the following:

```
sink.writeln("My guess is that your original number was ");
sink.writeln((result - 165)/100);
```

However, this will display two lines (instead of one):

```
My guess is that your original number was
1997
```

This happens because the `writeln` method outputs a string on a *separate* line. More precisely, it outputs a string followed by a *newline* character (also known as a *return*).

To output a string *without* a return, you can use another method, named `write`:

```
sink.write("My guess is that your original number was ");
sink.writeln((result - 165)/100);
```

The `writeln` statement

```
sink.writeln((result - 165)/100);
```

is just an abbreviation for outputting the expression value followed by a newline character. This statement has the same effect as the two `write` statements:

```
sink.write((result - 165)/100); sink.write(nl);
```

Since the newline character is *invisible*, it cannot be printed. So the only way we can refer to it in a program text is by giving it a *name*. The Java text program introduces the name `nl` for the newline character.

Notice that `nl` and `"nl"` are different kinds of symbols: `nl` is the *name* of a *character*, while `"nl"` is a *string* consisting of the letters n and l. The need to distinguish between names and strings is exactly the reason why strings are enclosed in quotes.

1.3.5   String Concatenation

To make your program text *readable*, you must, of course, make sure that the statements fit on a printed page. It may sometimes be necessary (or desirable) to break a long statement, like

```
sink.write("My guess is that your original number was ");
```

into shorter lines, such as

```
sink.write("My guess is that your
  original number was ");
```

Unfortunately, Java does *not* permit a *line break* in the middle of a string. But you can split the string

```
"My guess is that your original number was "
```

into two shorter strings

```
"My guess is that your"
" original number was "
```

and use a + operator to glue the strings together again:

```
sink.write("My guess is that your"
  + " original number was ");
```

The + operator tells the computer to combine the two strings into one before outputting it. This is called *string concatenation*. (The word *concatenate* means "to link together, as in a chain.")

1.3.6 Escape Sequences

The program really ought to display the word `guess` in quotation marks to show that there is no guessing involved:

```
My "guess" is that your original number was
```

So we must add two quotation marks inside the output string:

```
sink.write("My "guess" is that your"
  + " original number was ");
```

As it stands, this statement will be rejected by the compiler. Since programs use double quotes to show where a string *begins* and *ends*, a double quote cannot be used as a character *inside* a string.

Instead, we use the character combination \" to denote a double quote used as a string character. The character symbol \" is called an *escape sequence*.

We now have a correct output statement

```
sink.write("My \"guess\" is that your"
  + " original number was ");
```

1.3.7   Comments

As a final touch, it is helpful to include a *comment* in the program text to remind the reader what the program does:

```
/* "Guesses" a number selected by you. */
```

A comment begins with /* and ends with */ and is for the reader's benefit only. It has no effect on the execution of the program.

1.3.8   The Program "Trick"

Now, we have all the pieces of the program. The complete program, named trick, is shown below. The program terminates after closing *both* files.

Program 1.2 *Trick.*

```
/* "Guesses" a number selected by you. */

class trick extends basic
{ public static void main(String param[]) throws Exception
  { input source = new input();
    output sink = new output();
    sink.writeln("Think of a number");
    source.readln();
    sink.writeln("Multiply it by 5");
    source.readln();
    sink.writeln("Add 6");
    source.readln();
    sink.writeln("Multiply by 4");
    source.readln();
    sink.writeln("Add 9");
    source.readln();
    sink.writeln("Multiply by 5");
    source.readln();
    sink.writeln("Type the final result");
    int result = source.readint();
    sink.write("My \"guess\" is that your"
      + " original number was ");
    sink.writeln((result - 165)/100);
    source.close(); sink.close();
  }
}
```

1.3.9   Disk Input/Output

If you want Program 1.2 to use *disk files* for input/output (instead of keyboard and screen), all you have to do is to add a *string parameter* to each file constructor:

```
input source = new input("data");
output sink = new output("results");
```

The first statement opens an *existing* disk file, named `data`, for input. The second statement opens a *new* disk file, named `results`, for output. (Notice that the previous constructors for keyboard and screen files have *no* string parameters.)

Before running the program with disk input/output, you must use a text editor to type the `data` file:

◁
◁
◁
◁
◁
◁
199865◁

The file consists of six newline characters, followed by the integer `199865`, and a final newline character. Since newline characters are invisible on a printed page (and on the screen), I use the symbol ◁ to show you exactly where they occur in the input file.

1.3.10 Endless Execution

In the `data` file, the initial newline characters are necessary since the program includes six `readln` statements. If any of them are omitted, the computer will wait forever to input a (non-existing) newline character. This is an example of a program that fails to terminate because its input data and input statements do not match.[†]

1.3.11 More Terminology

The are two kinds of *methods*:

- A *function* is a method, such as `readint`, that yields a *value* when it is executed.

- A *procedure* is a method, such as `writeln`, that has *no value*.

[†]On Unix, you can *interrupt* endless execution of a program by pressing the `control` key and holding it down while typing `c`. This character combination is called `control-c`. On a Macintosh, hold down the `command` and `option` keys while pressing the `esc` key.

The execution of a method is called an *invocation* of the method. Functions and procedures are invoked differently:

- A *function designator* is an *expression* that denotes a function value.

  Example: `source.readint()`

- A *procedure statement* is a *statement* that denotes a procedure invocation.

  Example: `sink.writeln("Add 9");`

Method invocations are also known as function and procedure *calls*. A function call is said to *return* a value.

1.4   KEYWORDS AND NAMES

The words used in a program text are either keywords or names.

Keywords, such as `class` and `new`, have fixed meanings in the programming language and cannot be used for any other purpose. Table 1.1 shows all the keywords of Java.

Table 1.1   *Java Keywords.*

abstract	default	if	private	throw
boolean	do	implements	protected	throws
break	double	import	public	transient
byte	else	instanceof	return	try
case	extends	int	short	void
catch	final	interface	static	volatile
char	finally	long	super	while
class	float	native	switch	
const	for	new	synchronized	
continue	goto	package	this	

Names are introduced by programmers to denote entities, such as classes, methods, files, and variables. In programming languages, names are also known as *identifiers*.

A *name* consists of at least one letter, which may be followed by more letters and digits. A capital letter and the corresponding small letter are considered different letters.

The underscore _ is considered a letter. Consequently, a name can begin with an underscore or consist entirely of underscores! This absurd convention suggests that future language designers should pay less attention to what computers can handle and concentrate on inventing *readable notatation* for people.

Examples: correct names

```
i   LaTeX_2e   hello   Hello
```

Examples: incorrect names

```
2pm  new
```

The following *restrictions* apply to names and keywords:

- Keywords cannot be used as names.

- Names introduced in the main block must be distinct. (Later, I will define the exception to this general rule.)

- Line breaks cannot occur in the middle of keywords and names.

1.5 VARIABLES AND TYPES

Variables can store not only integers, but also characters and strings.

1.5.1 Integer Variables

An integer variable has an integer value.

The declarations

```
int sum = 1, old;
```

introduce an integer variable **sum**, *initialized* to 1, and another variable **old**, which is *uninitialized.*

The *assignment* statement

```
sum = sum + 2;
```

replaces the current value of the variable **sum** with a new value, defined by an expression, **sum + 2**.

The assignment takes place in two steps:

- First, the expression is evaluated by retrieving the current value of the variable (which is **1**) and adding **2** to it.

- Then the expression value **3** is assigned to the variable.

Since a variable can only hold one value at a time, an assignment *overwrites* the previous value of the variable. If you want to *save* the old value, it must be assigned to another variable *before* the assignment:

```
old = sum; sum = sum + 2;
```

The *operands* of an expression may be constants, variables, and subexpressions (possibly enclosed in parentheses).

Some *arithmetic operations* require two operands:

Operator	Operation	Example
+	addition	`adults + children`
-	subtraction	`result - 165`
*	multiplication	`10*sum`
/	division	`n/10`
%	modulus	`year%4`

Division yields an integer quotient; the fraction (if any) is ignored, and no rounding takes place. The *modulus* is the integer remainder of a division.

Example:

217 sec is **217/60** min and **217%60** sec, which is 3 min and 37 sec.

The following operations apply to single operands only:

Operator	Operation	Example
+	identity	`+200`
-	sign inversion	`-(10*amount)`

1.5.2   Character Variables

The value of a character variable is a character.

The declarations

```
char c = 's', d;
```

introduce two *character variables* c and d. The initial value of variable c is the letter s. The *character constant*

```
's'
```

is enclosed in single quotes to distinguish it from the string

```
"s"
```

The *space* character is denoted ' ' or sp. The *newline* character (also known as *return*) is named nl.

The assignment statement

```
d = c;
```

assigns the value of variable c to variable d without changing the value of c. Both variables now have the same value

```
's'
```

1.5.3 String Variables

The value of a string variable is a string.

Example:

```
String city = "Mexico City";
```

I have already explained how strings are concatenated by means of the + operator.

1.5.4 Escape Sequences

In character constants and strings, the following characters are represented by *escape sequences*:

Character	Escape sequence
'	\'
"	\"
\	\\

Examples:

```
'\''   '\"'   "It\'s \"ok\""   "\\"
```

1.5.5   The Type Concept

A *variable declaration* always includes a type symbol and a variable name.
Examples:

```
int number = 15; char c = 's'; String word = "stop";
```

The *type symbol* defines all the possible values that can be assigned to
the variable:

- Type int is the following set of integer values

  ```
  -2147483648, ..., -2, -1, 0, 1, 2, ..., 2147483647
  ```

- Type char is the set of available characters.

- Type String is the set of all possible character strings of finite length.

The use of data types clarifies the meaning of programs and enables a
compiler to check that the use of a variable is consistent with its type.

A program can assign an integer to an integer variable, say,

```
int number = 15;
```

But an attempt to assign a string to the same variable

```
int number = "stop";
```

is a *type error* that will be caught by the compiler.

1.6   MORE INPUT/OUTPUT

1.6.1   Characters

The input statement

```
char c = in.read();
```

reads the next character from an input file in and assigns it to variable c.
The output statement

```
out.write(c);
```

writes the character stored in variable c to an output file out.
To output a character, say, '*', followed by a newline character, use

```
out.writeln('*');
```

The statement

```
out.writeln();
```

outputs a newline character. This is an abbreviation for

```
out.write(nl);
```

Finally,

```
in.readnext();
```

reads the next character from an input file and *skips* it.

1.6.2 Strings

I will use three *string variables*

```
String name, word, line;
```

to input the line

```
Oh! That is terrible!◁
```

(or some of it) in four different ways.

The statement

```
name = in.readname();
```

inputs a string of letters and assigns it to the variable **name**. The input stops when the computer reaches the first exclamation mark. In this example, the statement has the same effect as the assignment

```
name = "Oh";
```

In general, the **readname** method inputs a string of consecutive letters, digits, and underscores.

If we use the **readword** method instead

```
word = in.readword();
```

the effect is equivalent to

```
word = "Oh!";
```

Spaces and newline characters are called *blanks*. The readword method inputs a string of consecutive, nonblank characters. In the above example, the input stops when it reaches the space after the "word" Oh!.

The program can also read the whole line

```
line = in.readline();
```

which, in this case, has the same effect as

```
line = "Oh! That is terrible!";
```

The **readline** method inputs a line (*including* the final **nl** character) and returns it (*without* the **nl**).

Finally, the **readln** method inputs and skips a line (including the **nl** character):

```
in.readln();
```

The **readname**, **readword**, and **readline** methods all *skip leading blanks*. So it makes no difference if the input line begins with, say, three spaces:

⊔⊔⊔Oh!⊔That⊔is⊔terrible!◁

The ⊔ and ◁ symbols are not part of the input file. I use them only to show where *spaces* and *newline* characters occur in the input.

You can also use

```
in.readblanks();
```

to input and skip consecutive blanks. (If the next input character is not a blank, this statement has no effect.)

1.6.3   Format Control

The output methods, discussed so far, do not support the printing of *tables* with *aligned columns*.

In 1980, about one million students received bachelor's degrees from American colleges and universities (Hacker 1983). The following block inputs the number of degrees in architecture and foreign languages, and outputs them as a small table:

```
{ int arch = in.readint(), lang = in.readint();
  out.writeln("Architecture " + arch);
  out.writeln("Foreign Languages " + lang);
}
```

The printed output

```
Architecture 9109
Foreign languages 11314
```

clearly needs some improvement. What I really want is something like this:

```
Architecture          9109
Foreign Languages    11314
```

Each table line consists of an *alphanumeric field* followed by a *numeric field*. The alphanumeric fields are 20 characters long:

```
Architecture⎵⎵⎵⎵⎵⎵⎵⎵
Foreign Languages⎵⎵⎵
```

and the numeric fields are 6 characters long:

```
⎵⎵9109
⎵11314
```

Here's how it's done:

```
{ out.write("Architecture", 20);
  out.writeln(arch, 6);
  out.write("Foreign languages", 20);
  out.writeln(lang, 6);
}
```

The write statement

```
out.write("Architecture", 20);
```

outputs the string `"Architecture"` as an *alphanumeric field* of 20 characters. The printed string is padded with *trailing spaces*.

Similarly, the write statement

```
out.writeln(arch, 6);
```

outputs the integer `9109` as a *numeric field* of 6 characters. The printed integer is extended with *leading spaces*.

The control of output to achieve a desired layout is called *format control*. By convention, *formatted strings* are *left-justified*, while *formatted numbers* are *right-justified*.

In general, a write statement

```
out.write(e, w);
```

outputs the value of an expression e with a field width defined by another expression w. The output value must be an integer, a character, a string, or a boolean (see 2.5). The field width must be an integer.

A single character is output with trailing spaces (if necessary).

The write variant

```
out.writeln(e, w);
```

outputs a newline character at the end of the output field.

1.7 PROGRAMMING EXERCISES

Exercise 1.1 Welcome

Write a Java program that displays the question:

```
What is your name?
```

You must now type your name on a single line, then press return. For example:

```
Jane Doe
```

The program inputs your name and displays the following greeting (which includes your name):

```
Welcome to Java, Jane Doe!
```

Exercise 1.2 Backwards Spelling

Write a Java program that asks you to:

```
Type a four-letter word that is
also a word if spelled backwards
```

If you type, say,

```
stop
```

followed by return, the program displays the (unhelpful) message

```
You decide if "pots" is a word
```

Exercise 1.3 Silly Jeopardy

Write a Java program that displays the answers to five questions and asks you what you think the questions are. The program begins by displaying the following:

```
The answer is: An anchor. What is the question?
```

You must now type a single line followed by return, for example:

```
Who is Peter Jennings?
```

The program responds as follows:

```
No, it's not: Who is Peter Jennings?
The question is: What's tattooed on Popeye's arm?
```

The program displays four more answers:

```
The Soviet Union.
The elephant.
Pink.
The goat.
```

and inputs four questions typed by you, one at a time. No matter what you type, the program contradicts you.

Exercise 1.4 Conversation

Write a Java program that displays one question at a time on the screen, inputs your answer from the keyboard, and outputs a brief (unimaginative) response. Here is an example of a conversation between the computer and you:

```
What is your name?
Jane Doe
Hi, Jane Doe. Where are you from?
California
I always wanted to visit California.
What kind of music do you like?
Classical
Classical is alright. How about jazz?
No
I see. Do computers worry you?
I hate computers
You say "I hate computers."
I'm sorry to hear that, but I enjoyed talking to you.
```

Exercise 1.5 Gasoline Prices

Write a Java program that enables tourists to compare U.S. and Danish prices of gasoline. The program asks you to type the U.S. price of regular gasoline in cents per gallon and displays the corresponding Danish price in orer per liter. (An ore is the smallest Danish coin: 1 krone = 100 orer.) Here is an example of the user's dialog with this program:

```
Type the U.S. price in cents/gallon
130
The corresponding Danish price is 226 orer/liter
```

Using the following conversion rules, the problem can be solved by integer arithmetic (without using fractions):

100 U.S. cents = 660 Danish orer
100 U.S. gallons = 379 liters

2

SIMPLE CHOICE

A simple program always performs the same sequence of operations when it runs. We will now explore programs that have a choice between different actions depending on the input data.

2.1   IF STATEMENTS

A program asks the question:

```
Approximately how many pennies are there
   in one U.S. pound of pennies?
Type your answer:
```

You already know how to program this:

```
{ input in = new input();
  output out = new output();
  out.writeln("Approximately how many pennies are there");
  out.writeln("  in one U.S. pound of pennies?");
  out.writeln("Type your answer:");
  int answer = in.readint();
  ...
}
```

It is probably too much to expect the user to know the exact answer, which (as far as I can tell) is 160 pennies. So let's settle for any value that is correct within 10%. In other words, any answer from 144 to 176 will do.

There are three possibilities:

- If the answer is less than 144, the program displays the message,
  `Too few - try again`

- If the answer is greater than 176, the response is,
  `Too many - try again`

- Any other answer is accepted as `Close enough!`

At this point, the program ends. To make another guess, you have to run it again.

Here is a situation in which a program must adapt its response to the input data. To handle this problem, we need a statement for *conditional execution*.

2.1.1 Conditional Execution

The *if statement*

```
if (answer < 144)
  out.writeln("Too few - try again");
else ...
```

has the following effect:

- If the value of the variable, `answer`, is less than 144, the output statement is executed.

- If the answer is *not* less than 144, the output statement is *skipped*, and the execution continues after the keyword `else`.

After `else`, you can write *any statement* you like. In particular, you can write *another* `if` statement:

```
if (answer < 144)
  out.writeln("Too few - try again");
else if (answer > 176)
  out.writeln("Too many - try again");
else ...
```

The program now behaves like this:

- If the answer is less than 144, the first output statement is executed.

- If the answer is not less than 144, the first output statement is skipped. There are now two more possibilities:

- if the answer is greater than 176, the second output statement is executed;

- otherwise, the second output statement is also skipped, and the execution continues after the final `else`.

After the final `else` you can again write *any statement* you like:

```
if (answer < 144)
  out.writeln("Too few - try again");
else if (answer > 176)
  out.writeln("Too many - try again");
else
  out.writeln("Close enough!");
```

In this example, I have combined two `if` statements to define a choice between three different output statements.

2.1.2 Constant Declarations

In a larger program with hundreds or thousands of lines, it is not advisable to include specific numbers, such as 144 and 176, in the middle of the program text. If you ever decide to change these constants, you may have to read the whole program text to find and edit them.

In our example, it is a good idea to define the *minimum* and *maximum* number of pennies as *named constants*:

```
int /* exact = 160, */ min = 144, max = 176;
```

Since the program doesn't use the *exact* value, I have included it as a comment only.

Technically speaking, these are initialized variables (and not constants). However, since the program leaves their values unchanged, they are *used* as named constants. (I will not bother you with Java's complicated notation for constant declarations.)

The rest of the program can now use the names, `min` and `max`, to refer to these bounds. If it becomes necessary to change the constant values, you only have to edit their declarations; the rest of the program can be left unchanged.

2.1.3   The Program "Pennies"

This completes the first conditional program:

Program 2.1 *Pennies.*

```
/* Asks the question: "Approximately how many pennies are
   there in one U.S. pound of pennies?" The answer must be
   within 10 % of the exact number.
*/

class pennies extends basic
{ public static void main(String param[]) throws Exception
  { input in = new input();
    output out = new output();
    out.writeln("Approximately how many pennies are there");
    out.writeln("  in one U.S. pound of pennies?");
    out.writeln("Type your answer:");
    int /* exact = 160, */ min = 144, max = 176,
      answer = in.readint();
    if (answer < min)
      out.writeln("Too few - try again");
    else if (answer > max)
      out.writeln("Too many - try again");
    else
      out.writeln("Close enough!");
    in.close(); out.close();
  }
}
```

2.2   STRING COMPARISON

I wrote a program that asks you to

   Name one of the world's 5 largest cities

If you answer Mexico City, the program responds with

   Yes, Mexico City is number 4 with a population of 15,525,000

An incorrect possibility is flatly rejected:

   No, Pasadena is not one of the 5 largest cities. Try again.

The program inputs your answer in a string variable:

   String city = in.readline();

If you type `Mexico City` (and press return), the `readline` method has the same effect as the assignment

```
city = "Mexico City";
```

The program first checks if your answer is `Tokyo`, which is the largest city:

```
if (city.equals("Tokyo"))
  out.writeln("Yes, Tokyo is number 1 with"
    + " a population of 26,518,000");
else ...
```

If the value of the variable `city` is `"Tokyo"`, the `writeln` statement is executed; otherwise, the execution continues after `else`, where the program looks for the second largest city:

```
else if (city.equals("New York"))
  out.writeln("Yes, New York is number 2 with"
    + " a population of 16,271,000");
else ...
```

2.2.1 Block Statements

You may find it tedious to write five similar output messages. You can avoid that by using two variables to hold the rank and population of a city:

```
int no; String pop;
if (city.equals("Tokyo"))
  { no = 1; pop = "26,518,000"; }
else if (city.equals("New York"))
  { no = 2; pop = "16,271,000"; }
else ...
```

If you chose `Tokyo`, the program executes the *block*

```
{ no = 1; pop = "26,518,000"; }
```

which assigns the values 1 and `"26,518,000"`, respectively, to the variables `no` and `pop`.

A block is a sequence of statements that are executed in the order written. You are already familiar with the `main` block of a program. Now, you see that a block can also be used as a *substatement* of an `if` statement. A block used as a statement is called a *block statement*.

2.2.2 Type Conversion

When the program has checked your answer, it uses the name, number, and population of the chosen city to put a response together:

```
out.writeln("Yes, " + city + " is number "
  + no + " with a population of " + pop);
```

First, the city name is _concatenated_ with two other strings to produce a single string, such as

```
"Yes, Mexico City is number "
```

This string is then concatenated with the city number in two steps:

1. The integer value of the city number, say, 4, is automatically converted to the corresponding string "4". This is called a _type conversion._

2. The string "4" is added at the end of the previous string:

   ```
   "Yes, Mexico City is number 4"
   ```

After two more concatenations, the final string

```
"Yes, Mexico City is number 4 with a population of 15,525,000"
```

is ready to be displayed.

This is all we need to complete the program.

2.2.3 The Program "The Largest Cities"

Program 2.2 _The Largest Cities._

```
/* Asks the user to name one of the World's
   five largest cities and displays its
   population (if the user is right).
*/

class cities extends basic
{ public static void main(String param[]) throws Exception
  { input in = new input();
    output out = new output();
    out.writeln("Name one of the world's 5"
      + " largest cities");
    String city = in.readline();
    int no = 6; String pop = "";
    if (city.equals("Tokyo"))
```

```
            { no = 1; pop = "26,518,000"; }
        else if (city.equals("New York"))
            { no = 2; pop = "16,271,000"; }
        else if (city.equals("Sao Paulo"))
            { no = 3; pop = "16,110,000"; }
        else if (city.equals("Mexico City"))
            { no = 4; pop = "15,525,000"; }
        else if (city.equals("Shanghai"))
            { no = 5; pop = "14,709,000"; }
        if (no <= 5)
            out.writeln("Yes, " + city + " is number "
              + no + " with a population of " + pop);
        else
            out.writeln("No, " + city + " is not one of"
              + " the 5 largest cities. Try again.");
        in.close(); out.close();
    }
}
```

Since the program depends on the value of the variable no, I have made sure that this variable also has a well-defined value if the city name is wrong. Program 2.2 handles this problem by initializing the variable no to 6 and leaving it unchanged if the chosen city is not one of the five largest.

Logically speaking, it is unnecessary to initialize the variable pop to an *empty string* "". The Java compiler recognizes that this variable is left uninitialized if the computer skips every block in the first if statement. But the compiler cannot tell that no value is needed in this case. So it forces you to add an unnecessary assignment statement. This illustrates how compilers can complicate programming if their designers try to be too clever.

I cannot resist quoting the immortal words of William Strunk (1959) about writing style:

> Omit needless words. Vigorous writing is concise. A sentence should contain no unnecessary words, a paragraph no unnecessary sentences, for the same reason that a drawing should have no unnecessary lines and a machine no unnecessary parts. This requires not that the writer make all his sentences short, or that he avoid all detail and treat his subject only in outline, but that every word tell.

This is equally sound advice for computer programming: *Omit needless statements!*

2.3   THE TYPE BOOLEAN

Now we must take a closer look at the programming concepts that make
conditional execution possible.

2.3.1   Boolean Values

The `if` statement

```
if (answer < min)
  out.writeln("Too few - try again");
```

includes a *condition*

```
answer < min
```

which may or may not be satisfied. This condition is an *assumption* that is
either *true* or *false*. If the `answer` is less than `min`, the assumption is true;
otherwise, it is false.

We will regard such an assumption as an *expression* that defines a *truth
value*. It is called a *boolean expression* in honor of the English mathematician
George Boole (Bell 1965). A boolean expression is either true or false. The
possible *boolean values* are denoted `true` and `false`. These constants are
said to be of type `boolean`.

The following table shows the boolean value of the previous expression
for different values of the answer:

answer	min	answer < min
100	144	true
150	144	false

2.3.2   Boolean Variables

You can declare a boolean variable and use it to record whether or not the
user estimates too few pennies in a U.S. pound:

```
boolean toofew;
if (answer < min) toofew = true;
else toofew = false;
```

These three lines can be replaced by a single assignment:

```
boolean toofew = (answer < min);
```

which is executed in two steps:

- First, the boolean expression, `answer < min`, is evaluated to obtain a value, which is either `true` or `false`.

- This value is then assigned to the boolean variable `toofew`.

2.3.3 Comparison Operators

The following boolean variable is used to record whether or not the user's estimate is exact:

```
int exact = 160;
boolean correct = (answer == exact);
```

The value of the boolean expression, `answer == exact`, is `true` if the user's answer and the exact amount are the same; otherwise, it is `false`. Notice the difference betweeen the *equality* operator `==` and the assignment operator `=`.

The *inequality* operator `!=` can be used to determine if the user's answer is *not equal* to the exact value:

```
boolean wrong = (answer != exact);
```

Here are the values of these expressions for two different answers:

answer	answer == exact	answer != exact
160	true	false
200	false	true

The *comparison operators* are listed below:

Operator	Operation	Example
<	less	hour < 11
>	greater	year > 1999
<=	less than or equal	min <= 59
>=	greater than or equal	month >= 1
==	equal	hour == 11
!=	not equal	day != 31

These operators are used to compare two operands of the same simple type. The types `int`, `char`, and `boolean` are called *simple types*.

It is a pity that Java does not use the equality operator for string comparison. If you could write

```
if (city == "Tokyo") ...
```

instead of

```
if (city.equals("Tokyo")) ...
```

there would one less (irrelevant) detail to remember. A programming language should not burden its users with different notations for the same concept. Sounds obvious, doesn't it? I wish that language designers felt the same way. *In programming, simplicity is not merely a desirable option. It is the main goal!*

2.3.4 Boolean Operators

Sometimes it is convenient to combine two comparisons into one, for example:

```
if ((min <= answer) & (answer <= max))
   out.writeln("Close enough");
```

The & operator is pronounced "and". So the if statement can be read as follows: if the answer is greater than or equal to min, *and* the answer is less than or equal to max, then the output statement is executed.

The boolean value of this *compound condition* can also be stored in a variable:

```
boolean close = (min <= answer) & (answer <= max);
```

The next example uses the | operator, which is pronounced "or"

```
boolean off = (answer < min) | (answer > max);
```

If the answer is less than min, *or* the answer is greater than max, then the value of the variable off is true; otherwise, it is false.

In general, a boolean expression of the form

```
x & y
```

uses two boolean operands, x and y, to compute a boolean result. If both operands have the value true, the result of the *and* operation is true; otherwise, the result is false.

The result of an *or* operation

```
x | y
```

is `true`, if *either* operand is `true`; otherwise, it is `false`.

The following table summarizes these computational rules for the *boolean operators* for all possible values of the operands:

x	y	x & y	x | y
false	false	false	false
false	true	false	true
true	false	false	true
true	true	true	true

If you want to determine if a boolean operand is `false`, you can use the `!` operator, which is pronounced "not"

```
if (!city.equals("Pasadena")) ...
```

This expression is only true if the city is *not* Pasadena. In other words, if

```
city.equals("Pasadena")
```

is `false` then

```
!city.equals("Pasadena")
```

must be `true`.

Conversely, if the city *is* Pasadena, then it is obviously false to say that it is *not* Pasadena. So, if

```
city.equals("Pasadena");
```

is `true`, then

```
!city.equals("Pasadena")
```

must be `false`.

This boils down to a simple computational rule: the result of a *not* operation

```
!x
```

is the "opposite" of the value of the boolean operand `x`:

x	!x
false	true
true	false

2.4   STRUCTURED STATEMENTS

One of the most powerful thinking tools is the idea of combining smaller
building blocks into larger units. The dictionary has a whole vocabulary
for this method of problem solving: *arrangement, combination, synthesis,
framework, structure,* and *composition.*

The idea of combining things permits you to divide complicated problems
into smaller problems that can be solved separately. This *divide and conquer*
approach to problem solving is particularly effective when you are combining
elements into new elements of the *same kind.* Why is that? Well, when things
are similar, there is less to understand and remember.

Since a programming language is a thinking tool, it is not surprising that
it exploits the idea of *combining smaller statements into larger statements.*

As an example, an `if` statement combines a boolean expression B and
two statements S1 and S2 into a single, larger statement:

```
if (B) S1 else S2
```

with the following effect: if B is `true`, then S1 is executed; else S2 is executed.

An even simpler form of composition is a *block statement*, which turns a
statement list SL into a single statement:

```
{ SL }
```

The *statement list* SL is a sequence of statements:

```
S1 S2 ... Sn
```

This combination of statements is so trivial that it hardly seems worth talking about. But without a block notation, you cannot easily specify that a
sequence of statements must be executed as a unit, say, if a condition B is
true:

```
if (B) { S1 S2 ... Sn }
```

So, we have two kinds of statements:

- Assignment and procedure statements are *simple statements,* which
  cannot be split into smaller statements.

- Block statements and `if` statements are *structured statements,* which
  are composed of smaller *substatements.*

The power of structured statements derives from the rule that *any* statement can be used as a substatement. This enables you to *combine statements freely* without arbitrary restrictions.

Incidentally, the rule that a statement ends with a *semicolon* applies only to simple statements (see 1.2).

2.5 THE EMPTY STATEMENT

A programming concept that almost seems superfluous is the *empty statement*, which consists of a semicolon only:

```
;
```

It does absolutely nothing! So, why do you need a notation for it? Well, in some situations, you don't want the computer to do anything. And, if you don't have a notation for this, you cannot express it in your programs.

Take, for example, the *short* form of the `if` statement

```
if (B) S
```

I can, of course, explain it as a new programming concept that is unrelated to anything else: if the boolean expression `B` is true, then the statement `S` is executed; otherwise, `S` is skipped.

However, if you already understand what the general `if` statement does, it is much easier to explain the short form as an abbreviation for a choice between a statement `S` and an empty statement:

```
if (B) S; else ;
```

2.5.1 Misplaced Semicolons

Be careful about where you put semicolons in a structured statement. The following `if` statement includes a misplaced semicolon after the `else`:

```
if (answer < min) toofew = true;
else; toofew = false;
```

This semicolon is interpreted as an *empty* statement. The (unexpected) effect is to make the `if` statement equivalent to

```
if (answer < min) toofew = true;
toofew = false;
```

2.6   BOOLEAN INPUT/OUTPUT

Here is a block that asks you a personal question and inputs your answer in a boolean variable:

```
{ out.writeln("Are you happy?");
  boolean yes = in.readboolean();
  out.write("Is that really ");
  out.write(yes);
  out.writeln("?");
}
```

- If you type `true` (and press return), the method `readboolean` returns the boolean value `true`. This value is assigned to the boolean variable `yes`. In that case, the block displays the response `Is that really true?`

- If you answer `false` to the question, the input statement assigns the boolean value `false` to the variable `yes`. The response to this answer is: `Is that really false?`

Notice the notational difference between the boolean constants `true` and `false`, and the corresponding string constants `"true"` and `"false"`.

Formatted booleans are right-justified (just like integers). The output statements

```
out.write(yes, 7); output.writeln(false, 7);
```

output the values `yes` and `false` as text fields of width 7, with leading spaces:

⊔⊔⊔true⊔⊔false◁

The second field is followed by a newline character.

2.7   PROGRAM ASSERTIONS

All programs must deal with *incorrect input*. Suppose my program inputs the current month:

```
int month = in.readint();
/* (1 <= month) & (month <= 12) */
```

I have added a comment to remind myself that it only makes sense to continue the execution of this program if the month is an integer from 1 to 12.

The boolean expression

```
(1 <= month) & (month <= 12)
```

is an *assertion* about the month which *should* be true at that point in the program. Unfortunately, this assertion is just a *comment* that has no effect on the execution.

If the month has a meaningless value, such as -57, I would prefer to display an error message

```
invalid month
```

and stop the program execution immediately. The Java text program defines a `halt` method for *abrupt termination*:

```
if (!((1 <= month) & (month <= 12)))
   halt("invalid month");
```

If the month is *not* an integer from 1 to 12, the program *halts* with an error message; otherwise, the if statement has no effect.

This assertion can also be checked as follows:

```
assume((1 <= month) & (month <= 12), "invalid month");
```

In general, an *assertion*

```
assume(b, e);
```

has no effect if the boolean expression `b` is `true`; otherwise, the program execution stops with the error message `e`. Notice that if the program execution continues beyond this statement, the assumption `b` is guaranteed to be satisfied.

The abbreviated form

```
assume(b);
```

displays the standard message `invalid assumption`, if it halts.

The `assume` method is part of the Java text program.

2.8   JAVA PITFALLS

My explanation of *strings* is only correct if you impose the following restriction on your use of this concept. Any program that violates this restriction can have unexpected results, which are not detected during compilation or execution.

● **Do not use comparison operators for strings.**

Example:

```
String city = in.readline();
if (city == "Mexico City") ...
```

Remedy: see 2.2.

2.9   PROGRAMMING EXERCISES

Exercise 2.1   Psychological Quiz

Write a Java program for a psychological quiz. The program displays the message:

```
Answer true or false to each question
```

The program then displays ten questions, one at a time, *exactly* as shown below:

```
 1. My work is usually fulfilling or interesting
 2. I have a good ability to relax
 3. I can enjoy happiness in little things easily
 4. I seldom envy other people
 5. My moods have great fluctuation
 6. I have a great desire to change either
    my location, family situation, or job
 7. I usually sleep well and don't feel
    tired in the morning
 8. I periodically "blow my top" without
    knowing the real reason
 9. I am usually a pessimistic person
10. I cannot have happiness
    without others being around me
```

After each question, the user must type either `true` or `false` (followed by a return). The program adds one point for each answer `true` to questions 1, 2, 3, 4, 7, and one for each answer `false` to questions 5, 6, 8, 9, 10. Then the total is multiplied by 10 to obtain a happiness score, which is displayed. For example:

```
Your happiness score is 60%
```

Exercise 2.2 U.S. Geography

Write a Java program that asks you five questions about U.S. geography. The program displays one question at a time on the screen. The first question is:

```
What state gets the most rain?
```

You must type the answer followed by return. If your answer is correct,

```
Hawaii
```

the program responds as follows

```
Yes, it's Hawaii
```

If the answer is incorrect, say,

```
Alaska
```

the program displays the message

```
No, it is not Alaska, it's Hawaii
```

The program then asks you four more questions, one at a time:

```
In what city is the Rose Bowl?
In what state is Yellowstone National Park?
What state is named for the Spanish word for red?
In what state is Fort Knox?
```

At the end, the program outputs your score, for example:

```
You answered 3 questions correctly
```

Exercise 2.3 Space Flights

Write a Java program that asks you,

```
In which years did the following space flights take place?
```

The program then displays the question:

```
First human orbital flight?
```

When you have typed the year (followed by return), say,

```
1961
```

the program tells you whether or not your answer is correct. The program then lists four more space flights and checks your answers, one at a time:

```
First lunar landing?
Viking 1 landed on Mars?
First space shuttle flight?
Hubble Space Telescope launched?
```

Exercise 2.4 Airmail

Write a Java program that computes the cost of sending an airmail parcel from the
United States to Estonia using the following rates (maximum weight limit 44 lbs):

```
First pound .......................... $13
Each additional pound up to 5 lbs ......   6
Each additional pound up to 10 lbs .....   5
Each additional pound over 10 lbs ......   4
```

The program displays the message

```
Type weight (lbs)
```

When you have typed the weight of a parcel (followed by a return), say,

```
12
```

the program displays the cost of sending the parcel:

```
The cost is $70
```

However, if the weight exceeds 44 lbs, the program responds with the message

```
Maximum weight limit 44 lbs
```

Use parcels of the following weights (in pounds) to *test* the program:

```
1    2    5    6    10    11    44    45
```

Exercise 2.5 Southern Caribbean

Write a Java program that helps you find an attractive vacation spot in the Southern
Caribbean using the following information:

Island	Non-stop flights	Beautiful beaches	Shopping
Barbados	✓	✓	✓
Grenada		✓	✓
St. Lucia	✓		✓
St. Vincent			
Trinidad	✓		
Tobago	✓	✓	

The program asks you three questions:

```
Are non-stop flights important?
Are beautiful beaches important?
Is shopping important?
```

When you have answered these questions, the program lists all the islands (if any)
that match your requirements. For example, if your answers are

```
true
false
true
```

the program suggests that you

```
Try Barbados or St. Lucia
```

3

MULTIPLE CHOICE

This chapter introduces the `switch` statement for programs that choose one of several actions depending on the value of an expression. It also describes programs that use random number generators to make unpredictable choices.

3.1 SWITCH STATEMENTS

The `if` statement defines a simple choice between *two alternatives*. However, by using `if` statements as substatements of other `if` statements, you can also program *multiple choice* (see Chapter 2).

I will now consider the special case in which a choice between, say, m actions is defined by one of the *natural numbers* 1, 2, . . . , m.

The first example is a program that inputs an all-figure *date* of the American form, say, 3/15/97, and outputs it in the form, `15 March 1997`.

The program inputs the `day`, `month`, and `year` in three integer variables. The two *slashes* are input and skipped by means of the `readnext` method.

```
{ input in = new input();
  output out = new output();
  out.writeln("Type a date, say, 3/15/97");
  int month = in.readint();
  in.readnext();
  int day = in.readint();
  in.readnext();
  int year = in.readint();
    ...
}
```

What happens if the input is not a valid date, say, 1/32/-1? The only thing a program can do is to reject a date that doesn't make sense. There are, of course, limits to how much *consistency checking* one should put into a small program.

It seems reasonable to check that the day is a natural number from 1 to 31. It would be all right to test this assumption as follows

```
assume((1 <= day) & (day <= 31)), "invalid day");
```

However, if the day is incorrect, the abrupt termination prevents the program from checking the rest of the input. This violates another programming principle:

- *A program should detect as many input errors as possible in a single run.*

Otherwise, the user is forced to run the program several times with the same incorrect input.

Incidentally, the same principle applies to *compiler design*. The input to a compiler is a program text, which often includes formal errors. The compiler attempts to find as many programming errors as possible in a single compilation. The compiler must do that without producing meaningless error messages or crashing, even if the input is today's newspaper (instead of a programming text). The problem of *error recovery* is one of the main challenges of compiler design (Brinch Hansen 1985).

Returning now to our example: the program can recover from an invalid day and continue its execution, simply by replacing the day by the string, "day?". Using this idea, the invalid date 1/32/-1 will be output as

```
day? January year?
```

We can now output the day (followed by a space):

```
if ((1 <= day) & (day <= 31))
  out.write(day);
else out.write("day?");
out.write(' ');
```

As far as the name of the month goes, there are 13 possibilities (yes, 13):

```
if (month == 1) out.write("January");
else if (month == 2) out.write("February");
else if (month == 3) out.write("March");
else if (month == 4) out.write("April");
```

```
else if (month == 5) out.write("May");
else if (month == 6) out.write("June");
else if (month == 7) out.write("July");
else if (month == 8) out.write("August");
else if (month == 9) out.write("September");
else if (month == 10) out.write("October");
else if (month == 11) out.write("November");
else if (month == 12) out.write("December");
else out.write("month?");
```

Although `if` statements can be combined to express *any* multiple choice, it can be argued that a multiple choice based on the value of a natural number occurs so often that it makes sense to have a notation for this *special case*.

The following *switch statement* uses the *number* of the month to output the *name* of the month:

```
switch (month)
  { case  1: out.write("January"); break;
    case  2: out.write("February"); break;
    case  3: out.write("March"); break;
    case  4: out.write("April"); break;
    case  5: out.write("May"); break;
    case  6: out.write("June"); break;
    case  7: out.write("July"); break;
    case  8: out.write("August"); break;
    case  9: out.write("September"); break;
    case 10: out.write("October"); break;
    case 11: out.write("November"); break;
    case 12: out.write("December"); break;
    default: out.write("month?"); break;
  }
```

The `switch` statement defines a choice between 13 output statements:

- If the `month` is equal to, say, 3, then the output statement labeled `case` 3 is executed:

```
out.write("March");
```

- If the `month` is not equal to any of `case` numbers 1, 2, ... , 12, the `default` case is executed:

```
out.write("month?");
```

In general, a `switch` statement

```
switch (e)
  { case c1: SL1 break;
    case c2: SL2 break;
       ...
    case cm: SLm break;
    default: SLn break;
  }
```

is a structured statement that defines a choice between m statement lists SL1, SL2, ... , SLm. The choice depends on the value of a *case expression* e, which must be of type int (or char). The *case numbers* c1, c2, ... , cm must be distinct constants of the same type as e.

A switch statement is executed in two steps: (1) first, the case expression e is evaluated to obtain a case value; (2) there are now two possibilities:

- If the case value is equal to one of the case numbers, say, ci, then the corresponding statement list SLi is executed.

- If the case value is not equal to any of the case numbers, the default statement list SLn is executed. (If it is superfluous, the default case may be omitted.)

This explanation of the switch statement deliberately ignores some of its (unnecessary) complexity.

3.1.1   The Program "Convert Date"

The rest of the date conversion program is straightforward:

Program 3.1 Convert Date.

```
/* 1. Inputs an all-figure date of the American
      form, say, 3/15/97.
   2. Checks that the day is between 1 and 31,
      the month is between 1 and 12, and the
      year is between 0 and 99.
   3. Outputs the date in the standard form,
      such as, 15 March 1997.
*/

class convertdate extends basic
{ public static void main(String param[]) throws Exception
  { input in = new input();
    output out = new output();
    out.writeln("Type a date, say, 3/15/97");
    int month = in.readint();
```

```
        in.readnext();
        int day = in.readint();
        in.readnext();
        int year = in.readint();
        if ((1 <= day) & (day <= 31))
          out.write(day);
        else out.write("day?");
        out.write(' ');
        switch (month)
          { case  1: out.write("January"); break;
            case  2: out.write("February"); break;
            case  3: out.write("March"); break;
            case  4: out.write("April"); break;
            case  5: out.write("May"); break;
            case  6: out.write("June"); break;
            case  7: out.write("July"); break;
            case  8: out.write("August"); break;
            case  9: out.write("September"); break;
            case 10: out.write("October"); break;
            case 11: out.write("November"); break;
            case 12: out.write("December"); break;
            default: out.write("month?"); break;
          }
        out.write(' ');
        if ((0 <= year) & (year <= 99))
          out.writeln(1900 + year);
        else out.writeln("year?");
        in.close(); out.close();
      }
    }
```

3.2 PROGRAM TESTING

How do you *test* if this program works? You run it with some input and check that the output is correct. Fair enough, but how do you select the *test input?*

You can sit down at a terminal, scratch your head, and say to yourself: suppose I try today's date and then my birthday. However, it is very unlikely that a few "typical" dates, chosen at random, will test your program systematically. The program may still give wrong answers (or crash) for other dates. In short,

- *Random testing is unreliable.*

The most systematic testing method is clearly to try the program for all possible input dates. However, except for the most trivial programs

- *Exhaustive testing is impractical.*

In another book, I described the seemingly trivial problem of testing the addition unit of a computer for all possible combinations of two numbers (Brinch Hansen 1973):

> If we were to test the addition of two decimal numbers of 10 digits each exhaustively, it would require 10^{20} executions of a program loop of say, 10 μs, or, all in all, 30 million years. The only way to reduce this time is to use our knowledge of the internal *structure* of the adder. If we know that it consists of 10 identical components, each capable of adding two digits and a carry, we also know that it is sufficient to test each component separately with $10 \times 10 \times 2$ combinations of input digits. This insight immediately reduces the number of test cases to 2000 and brings the total test time down to only 1/50 of a second.

Most computer programs are much more complicated than a hardware adder. Since exhaustive testing is out of the question for most hardware circuits, it doesn't work for programs either.

Returning to the problem of testing the correctness of Program 3.1, we must accept that such a test is impossible, if all we know is that the program is a *black box* that converts a date by unknown magic.

However, if we take advantage of the *structure* of the program text, we can test the program systematically in reasonable time. But we must *select the test input systematically.* The least you can do is to

- *Make sure that each program statement is executed at least once.*

If you look at Program 3.1, you will see that the following *unconditional statements* will be executed for *any* input date:

```
√ input in = new input();
√ output out = new output();
√ out.writeln("Type a date, say, 3/15/97");
√ int month = in.readint();
√ in.readnext();
√ int day = in.readint();
√ in.readnext();
√ int year = in.readint();
    ...
√ out.write(' ');
    ...
√ out.write(' ');
    ...
√ in.close(); out.close();
```

Start a list of test input by writing down any date, for example, 1/1/0 (that is, January 1, 1900). Then write a check mark √ next to each of these statements to indicate that you have planned a test case for them.

- *In an* `if` *statement, both substatements must be tested.*

This requires two test cases, which make the boolean expression `true` and `false`, respectively.

The following table shows two possible test inputs for the first `if` statement:

(1 <= day) & (day <= 31)	test input
false	1/0/0
true	1/1/0

Now go ahead and mark the `if` statement as being ready for testing:

```
√ if ((1 <= day) & (day <= 31))
√   out.writeln(day);
√ else out.writeln("day?");
```

However, in this case, we can afford to be slightly more systematic and test the boolean expression for all possible values of the two comparisons of the day:

1 <= day	day <= 31	test input
false	false	(impossible)
false	true	1/0/0
true	false	1/32/0
true	true	1/1/0

I remark in passing that it is impossible for an integer to be both less than 1 and greater than 31. So, the first test case can never occur.

To test the `switch` statement and its substatements, you need a date for each month, and at least one invalid month for the default case. Write down the following sequence of test data

```
     1/1/0       2/2/1    3/3/33   4/4/44     5/5/55
    6/6/66      7/7/77    8/8/88   9/9/99   10/10/10
  11/11/11   12/11/13    13/1/0
```

and put a check mark next to the corresponding substatements:

```
√ case  1: out.write("January"); break;
√ case  2: out.write("February"); break;
```

```
√ case  3: out.write("March"); break;
√ case  4: out.write("April"); break;
√ case  5: out.write("May"); break;
√ case  6: out.write("June"); break;
√ case  7: out.write("July"); break;
√ case  8: out.write("August"); break;
√ case  9: out.write("September"); break;
√ case 10: out.write("October"); break;
√ case 11: out.write("November"); break;
√ case 12: out.write("December"); break;

√ default: out.write("month?"); break;
```

For the final **if** statement, select test cases for all possible boolean values
of the two comparisons of the year:

0 <= year	year <= 99	test input
false	false	(impossible)
false	true	1/1/-1
true	false	1/1/100
true	true	1/1/0

and mark the statements tested by this input:

```
√ if ((0 <= year) & (year <= 99))
√    out.writeln(1900 + year);

√ else out.writeln("year?");
```

Altogether, you now have 18 input dates. When you have run the program with these test cases, every statement has been executed at least once.

- *If a test case reveals a programming error, use the corresponding input
  to locate an incorrect statement.*

Let's say the test input is 10/10/10, but the output is 10 November
1910. Then you already know (without looking at the switch statement),
that the following case is wrong:

```
case 10: out.write("November"); break;
```

After changing the name of the tenth month to "October", you run the same
tests again.

- *Repeat the testing and editing of the program with the same input until
  all the output is correct.*

When the program works, it would seem that you no longer need the test input. However, it would be a mistake to throw the test input away:

- If you ever decide to *extend* the program with new features, it is wise to run all previous tests of the program again to verify that the changes have no influence on the correctness of the original statements.

- If you decide to *move* the program to another computer that uses a different Java compiler, it may be necessary to test the program again from scratch.

This brings me to another rule of testing:

- *The documentation of a program should include a list of systematic test cases.*

To illustrate this point, I have included the test cases in the initial comment of Program 3.1:

```
/* 1. Inputs an all-figure date of the American
      form, say, 3/15/97.
   2. Checks that the day is between 1 and 31,
      the month is between 1 and 12, and the
      year is between 0 and 99.
   3. Outputs the date in the standard form,
      such as, 15 March 1997.

   Test cases:

       1/1/0      2/2/1    3/3/33  4/4/44     5/5/55
       6/6/66     7/7/77   8/8/88  9/9/99  10/10/10
    11/11/11  12/11/13     0/1/1  13/1/0     1/0/0
       1/32/0     1/1/-1  1/1/100
*/
```

This method of program testing was invented by Naur (1992). If you think it works for small examples only, I can only say that I have used it for over 35 years to test compilers and operating systems of thousands of lines. After systematic testing, these programs were more reliable than the hardware on which they ran!

3.3   RANDOM CHOICE

In the date conversion program, the choices between different actions are completely determined by the input date. If you run the program several times with the same input, it will always make exactly the same choices. They are called *predictable* or *deterministic choices*.

Sometimes a program must make arbitrary choices. This is typical of programs that play games or simulate the real world (or imaginary ones). Such programs make *unpredictable* or *non-deterministic choices*. Consequently, they rarely repeat the same behavior twice in a row.

An example is a program that displays the title of an English novel and asks you to type the full name of the author. The novel is chosen at random from a list of five titles.

The first time you run this program, it may ask you

```
Who wrote the novel "The Color Purple"?
Type the author's full name
```

If your answer is correct, the program displays the message

```
Alice Walker is correct!
```

and terminates; otherwise, it suggests that you try again.

If you run the program again, it will probably display the title of another novel.

The program uses a random number to make an arbitrary choice between five novels. This number is generated by a class, named **random**, which is part of the Java text program.

First, the program opens a new *random number generator*, named **chance**, that produces random numbers from 1 to 5 only:

```
random chance = new random(1, 5);
```

The statement

```
int novel = chance.readint();
```

inputs a random integer in a variable, named **novel**.

If you run the program several times, the number of the selected novel will always be 1, 2, 3, 4, or 5. Which of the five numbers you will obtain in a particular execution is completely unpredictable.

If you could run this program an infinite number of times, each of the five novels would be equally likely to be selected. Since you cannot run the program forever, there will be variations in the number of times each novel is selected. If you were able to run the program 50,000 times, you might find that each novel was selected anywhere from 9,900 to 10,100 times. As you can see, the program comes close to the mathematical ideal of selecting each novel with the same probability of 1/5. In mathematical terminology, the 50,000 random numbers are practically *uniformly distributed* from 1 to 5.

Program 3.2 uses a `switch` statement to select a novel at random.

Program 3.2 *Authors.*

```
/* Displays the title of an English novel and
   asks the user to type the full name of the
   author. The novel is chosen randomly from
   a list of five titles.

   An example (showing the output only):

      Who wrote the novel "The Color Purple"?
      Type the author's full name
      Alice Walker is correct!
*/

class authors extends basic
{ public static void main(String param[]) throws Exception
  { input in = new input();
    output out = new output("results");
    random chance = new random(1, 5);
    String author = "", title = "";
    int novel = chance.readint();
    switch (novel)
      { case 1:
          title = "The Bell";
          author = "Iris Murdoch"; break;
        case 2:
          title = "The Color Purple";
          author = "Alice Walker"; break;
        case 3:
          title = "The Golden Notebook";
          author = "Dorris Lessing"; break;
        case 4:
          title = "Murder on the Orient Express";
          author = "Agatha Christie"; break;
        case 5:
          title = "Ship of Fools";
          author = "Katherine Anne Porter"; break;
      }
    out.writeln("Who wrote the novel \"" + title + "\"?");
    out.writeln("Type the author's full name");
    String answer = in.readline();
    if (answer.equals(author))
      out.writeln(answer + " is correct!");
    else
```

```
        out.writeln(answer + " is incorrect. Try again.");
      in.close(); out.close(); chance.close();
    }
  }
```

Notice again how the compiler forces you to initialize the name of the author and the title of the novel with *empty strings*, which are completely unnecessary:

```
String author = "", title = "";
```

3.4   PROGRAMMING STYLE

Up to this point, I have discussed how to use a programming language (in this case, Java) correctly. Now, I will go beyond the rules of the language and offer some advice on the question of programming style.

3.4.1   Readable Names

What makes some programs easier to understand than others? Well, to begin with it is essential to

- *Use readable variable names that remind the reader of their purpose.*

Most variable names in Program 3.2 are readable in that sense:

```
answer    author    chance    novel    title
```

- *Abbreviated names should be long enough to suggest what they stand for.*

The abbreviated file names

```
in    out
```

are acceptable mainly because they are followed by more readable method names. For example, `in.readline()` or `out.close()`.

You should normally

- *Avoid single-letter names.*

They may be easy to type, but, since they don't mean anything, they just make programs very hard to understand.

This is what Program 3.2 looks like if every variable name consists of a single letter only:

```
class authors extends basic
{ public static void main(String param[]) throws Exception
  { input i = new input();
    output o = new output();
    random c = new random(1, 5);
    String a = "", t = "";
    int n = c.readint();
    switch (n)
      { case 1:
          t = "The Bell";
          a = "Iris Murdoch"; break;
        case 2:
          t = "The Color Purple";
          a = "Alice Walker"; break;
        case 3:
          t = "The Golden Notebook";
          a = "Dorris Lessing"; break;
        case 4:
          t = "Murder on the Orient Express";
          a = "Agatha Christie"; break;
        case 5:
          t = "Ship of Fools";
          a = "Katherine Anne Porter"; break;
      }
    o.writeln("Who wrote the novel \"" + t + "\"?");
    o.writeln("Type the author's full name");
    String b = i.readline();
    if (b.equals(a))
      o.writeln(b + " is correct!");
    else
      o.writeln(b + " is incorrect. Try again.");
    i.close(); o.close(); c.close();
  }
}
```

The only thing that saves this program from being completely incomprehensible is that the text strings still have to be readable to make sense to the user at the terminal.

The lesson is clear:

- *Programs should be easy to read, but not necessarily easy to write!*

3.4.2 Program Indentation

A program text has a *hierarchical structure* in the sense that some statements include substatements, which, in turn, may have further substatements. The program text should clearly show the hierarchical relationships between the statements.

- *Use indentation to show the program structure.*

The following outline of the **main** block of Program 3.2 illustrates what I mean:

```
{ input in = new input();
  ...
  switch (novel)
    { case 1:
        title = "The Bell";
        author = "Iris Murdoch"; break;
      ...
      case 5:
        title = "Ship of Fools";
        author = "Katherine Anne Porter"; break;
    }
  out.writeln("Who wrote the novel \"" + title + "\"?");
  ...
  if (answer.equals(author))
    out.writeln(answer + " is correct!");
  else
    out.writeln(answer + " is incorrect. Try again.");
  in.close(); out.close();
}
```

In this example, I have used three rules of indentation:

- *In a block, every statement begins in the same column.*

- *In a structured statement, every substatement is indented by two spaces.*

- *The opening and closing braces of a block are aligned in the same column.*

To show the importance of using indentation consistently, I have rewritten Program 3.2 without any indentation whatsoever. Notice how difficult it is to recognize matching braces when they are not aligned.

```
class authors extends basic{
public static void main(String param[]) throws Exception{
input in = new input();
output out = new output();
random chance = new random(1, 5);
String author = "", title = "";
int novel = chance.readint();
switch (novel) {
case 1: title = "The Bell";
author = "Iris Murdoch"; break;
```

```
case 2: title = "The Color Purple";
author = "Alice Walker"; break;
case 3: title = "The Golden Notebook";
author = "Dorris Lessing"; break;
case 4: title = "Murder on the Orient Express";
author = "Agatha Christie"; break;
case 5: title = "Ship of Fools";
author = "Katherine Anne Porter"; break; }
out.writeln("Who wrote the novel \"" + title + "\"?");
out.writeln("Type the author's full name");
String answer = in.readline();
if (answer.equals(author))
out.writeln(answer + " is correct!"); else
out.writeln(answer + " is incorrect. Try again.");
in.close(); out.close(); chance.close(); }}
```

3.4.3 Final Remarks

It seems appropriate to end this discussion of programming style with two quotations. The first one is from Brinch Hansen (1973):

> I have stressed the need for simplicity in programming. I cannot accept the viewpoint that the construction of programs with a pleasant structure is an academic exercise that is irrelevant or impractical to use in real life. Simplicity of structure is not just an aesthetic pursuit—It is the key to survival in programming! Large systems can only be fully understood and tested if they can be studied in small, simple parts at many levels of detail.

Needless to say, it takes more than simplistic rules of style to make you a first-rate writer or programmer. Listen to what Peter Naur (1992) has to say about the difficulties of writing and programming:

> The most basic fact about natural style...is that good writing is very difficult, even for persons who have complete mastery of everyday spoken language. Good style is achieved only through insight, practice, and effort. By analogy, we can expect good programming style to remain a combination of sound principles, talent, and work, and that the fight against poor style is never ending.

3.5 JAVA PITFALLS

My explanation of `switch` statements is only correct if you impose the following restriction on your use of this concept. Any program that violates this restriction can have unexpected results, which are not detected during compilation or execution.

UNIVERSITY OF HERTFORDSHIRE LRC

- **Do not omit breaks in switch statements.**

Example:

```
switch (month)
  { case  1: out.write("January");
    case  2: out.write("February");
    case  3: out.write("March");
    case  4: out.write("April");
    case  5: out.write("May");
    case  6: out.write("June");
    case  7: out.write("July");
    case  8: out.write("August");
    case  9: out.write("September");
    case 10: out.write("October");
    case 11: out.write("November");
    case 12: out.write("December");
    default: out.write("month?");
  }
```

Instead, put a **break** after every case statement list (see Program 3.1).

3.6 PROGRAMMING EXERCISES

Exercise 3.1 Tomorrow's Date

Write a Java program that displays the message

    Type month/day/year

and inputs a date of this form from the keyboard:

- If the user types a date between 1/1/00 and 12/30/99, say, 6/30/97, the program displays the date of the following day on the screen, say, 7/1/97.

- If the user types an invalid date, say, 1/32/97, the program displays the message, Invalid date.

Note: The years 04, 08, 12, . . ., 96 are *leapyears.*

Use the following valid and invalid dates to *test* the program:

```
    1/1/00    2/28/00    2/29/96    2/28/97    3/30/97
   4/29/97    5/31/97    6/30/97    7/15/97    8/16/97
   9/17/97   10/18/97   11/19/97   12/31/98   12/30/99
    1/0/97    1/32/97    2/29/00     0/1/97    13/1/97
   1/1/-1    1/1/100   12/31/99
```

Exercise 3.2 Clockwork

Write a Java program that behaves like the clockwork of a digital watch. The program displays the following message on the screen:

```
Type day hour min sec am (or pm)
```

If the user types a valid day of the week and time of day, say,

```
Sa 11 59 59 pm
```

the clockwork advances by *one second* and displays the correct day and time at that point, say,

```
Su 12 0 0 am
```

The program reports if the user types an invalid day or time.

Use the following valid and invalid cases to *test* the program:

```
Su  1  0  0 am   Mo  2  1 58 am   Tu  9 58 59 am   We 10 59 59 am
Th 11 59 59 am   Fr 11 59 59 pm   Sa 11 59 59 pm   Su 12 59 59 pm
Sy  1  0  0 am   Su  0  0  0 am   Mo 13  0  0 am   Tu  1 -1  0 am
We  1 60  0 am   Th  1  0 -1 am   Fr  1  0 60 am   Sa  1  0  0 pn
```

Exercise 3.3 Writing Test

Write a Java program that does the following: first, the program displays the following writing test on the screen exactly as shown below (Barasch 1991):

```
"Though theirs no historical documentation,
it's not too hard to imagine how pasta was
invented."

What correction should be made to this sentence?
  1  Replace "Though" with "Although"
  2  Replace "theirs" with "there's"
  3  Change "it's" to "its"
  4  Change "was" to "is"
  5  No correction is necessary
```

Then, the program displays the message

```
The answer is
```

and inputs an integer from 1 to 5 from the keyboard.

Finally, the program displays the sentence again with the correction selected by the user. If the user, for example, typed the number

```
4
```

the sentence is displayed again with the word was changed to is:

```
"Though theirs no historical documentation,
it's not too hard to imagine how pasta is
invented."
```

Exercise 3.4 Spell Number

Write a Java program that inputs a number from 1 to 999 from the keyboard and spells out the number on the display. For example:

```
  5    five
 13    thirteen
 20    twenty
 46    forty-six
700    seven hundred
986    nine hundred and eighty-six
```

Use the following numbers to *test* the program:

```
  1    2    3    4    5    6    7    8    9
 11   12   13   14   15   16   17   18   19
 10   20   30   40   50   60   70   80   99
100  200  300  400  500  600  707  880  999
```

Exercise 3.5 U.S. Vice Presidents

Write a Java program that displays information about one of the following U.S. Vice Presidents:

Inaugurated	Name	Birthplace	Year
1953	Richard M. Nixon	Yorba Linda, CA	1913
1961	Lyndon B. Johnson	Johnson City, TX	1908
1965	Hubert H. Humphrey	Wallace, SD	1911
1969	Spiro T. Agnew	Baltimore, MD	1918
1973	Gerald R. Ford	Omaha, NE	1913
1974	Nelson A. Rockefeller	Bar Harbor, ME	1908
1977	Walter F. Mondale	Ceylon, MN	1928
1981	George Bush	Milton, MA	1924
1989	Dan Quayle	Indianapolis, IN	1947
1993	Al Gore	Washington, DC	1948

The program asks you to type an inauguration year and displays the name of the corresponding Vice President. The program then asks if you want to know more. If you answer yes, the program also shows when and where the Vice President was born. Here is an example of a dialog with this program:

```
Type inauguration year
1977
Walter F. Mondale
Do you want to know more?
yes
Born 1928 in Ceylon, MN.
```

You decide how the program should respond to an incorrect inauguration year.

SIMPLE REPETITION

This chapter explains how statements can be executed repeatedly by means of `for` statements.

4.1 FOR STATEMENTS

In our daily lives we depend on a wide variety of machines: clocks, washing machines, lawn mowers, thermostats, telephones, cars, elevators, slot machines, and, of course, computers. The most important property of a machine is that it can perform the same operations over and over again.

The programming concepts I have used so far are severely limited since they do *not* permit you to write *any program* that makes a computer repeat the same operations. It is time to remove this restriction and explore *repeated execution*.

4.1.1 Coin Tossing

I will illustrate the simplest form of repetition by writing a program that simulates coin tossing. Here is an example of the output of this program:

```
50 coin tosses:
HTHHHHTTHHHTTHHTTTTHTTHHHHTTTHTHTHTHHTHTTTHTTTHTHTTH
24 heads, 26 tails
```

The result of each toss is either a head (H) or a tail (T). In this run, the program generated 24 heads and 26 tails. The number of heads and tails will normally vary from one execution of the program to another.

This programming problem raises two questions:

- How do you simulate a coin toss?

- How do you repeat a coin toss 50 times?

The coin tosses are simulated by means of a *random number* generator, named `toss`. Two integer variables, initialized to zero, are used to count the number of `heads` and `tails`:

```
random toss = new random(1, 2);
int heads = 0, tails = 0;
```

I use a function call `toss.readint()` to generate a random integer, which is either 1 or 2. In the long run, each of these numbers will occur with (roughly) the same probability. Consequently, we can interpret a 1 as a *head*, and a 2 as a *tail*.

A single coin toss is now easy to program:

```
if (toss.readint() == 1)
   { out.write("H"); heads = heads + 1; }
else
   { out.write("T"); tails = tails + 1; }
```

It would be nice if you could repeat this statement 50 times by writing something like

```
repeat 50 times
   if (toss.readint() == 1)
     { out.write("H"); heads = heads + 1; }
   else
     { out.write("T"); tails = tails + 1; }
```

Strangely enough, most programming languages, including Java, do not have a notation for this special case. In Java, you can express it as follows:

```
for (int trial = 1; trial <= 50; trial++)
   if (toss.readint() == 1)
     { out.write("H"); heads = heads + 1; }
   else
     { out.write("T"); tails = tails + 1; }
```

This *for statement* consists of

- A variable, named `trial`, which the computer uses to count from 1 to 50. It is called the *control variable* of the `for` statement.

- An `if` statement which simulates a single coin toss. This substatement is known as the *body* of the `for` statement.

The effect of the `for` statement is to execute the body 50 times. In each trial, the `if` statement generates a fresh random number.

A single execution of the body is called an *iteration*. Since the number of iterations is fixed at the beginning of the `for` statement, this is known as *bounded repetition*. Due to the cyclic nature of iteration, a repetitive statement is also known as a *loop*.

Here is the complete coin tossing program:

Program 4.1 *Coin Tossing.*

```
/* Simulates a fixed number of coin tosses */

class coins extends basic
{ public static void main(String param[]) throws Exception
  { output out = new output("results");
    random toss = new random(1, 2);
    int times = 50;
    out.write(times);
    out.writeln(" coin tosses:");
    int heads = 0, tails = 0;
    for (int trial = 1; trial <= times; trial++)
      if (toss.readint() == 1)
        { out.write("H"); heads = heads + 1; }
      else
        { out.write("T"); tails = tails + 1; }
    out.writeln();
    out.write(heads); out.write(" heads, ");
    out.write(tails); out.writeln(" tails");
    out.close();
  }
}
```

4.2 NESTED REPETITION

Programs that print lines and squares illustrate the difference between *one-* and *two-dimensional repetition*.

To output a *line* of five asterisks

```
*****
```

you can use a single `for` statement followed by a `writeln` statement:

```
{ for (int j = 1; j <= 5; j++)
    out.write("*");
  out.writeln();
}
```

Since the control variable j is used only to repeat the **write** statement five times, there is no particular reason to give it a more meaningful name.

This **for** statement is equivalent to the following block:

```
{ int j;
  j = 1; out.write("*");
  j = 2; out.write("*");
    . . .
  j = 5; out.write("*");
  out.writeln();
}
```

A more interesting problem is to print a *square* of asterisks:

```
*****
*****
*****
*****
*****
```

This figure consists of five lines of five asterisks each. However, it looks more like a rectangle than a square. Well, that is because on printed paper, the spaces between characters on the same line are smaller than the spaces between lines.

This minor flaw can be corrected by outputting a *space* after each asterisk:

```
* * * * *
* * * * *
* * * * *
* * * * *
* * * * *
```

We need a second **for** statement to print the same line five times:

```
for (int i = 1; i <= 5; i++)
    . . .
```

Notice, that the two **for** statements use *different* control variables i and j.

The last step is to replace the ellipsis points . . . by the previous block, which prints a single line:

```
for (int i = 1; i <= 5; i++)
  { for (int j = 1; j <= 5; j++)
      out.write("* ");
    out.writeln();
  }
```

These *nested* statements have the same effect as the following nested blocks:

```
{ int i, j;
  i = 1;
  { j = 1; out.write("* ");
    j = 2; out.write("* ");
       . . .
    j = 5; out.write("* ");
    out.writeln();
  }
  i = 2;
  { j = 1; out.write("* ");
    j = 2; out.write("* ");
       . . .
    j = 5; out.write("* ");
    out.writeln();
  }
     . . .

  i = 5;
  { j = 1; out.write("* ");
    j = 2; out.write("* ");
       . . .
    j = 5; out.write("* ");
    out.writeln();
  }
}
```

For every single iteration of the outer **for** statement, the inner **for** statement performs the **write** statement five times and the **writeln** statement once. Since the outer **for** statement performs five iterations, the net effect is to output 5×5 asterisks and five *returns*.

What we have here is *two-dimensional counting*, where the control variables step through the following pairs of values (i,j), one line at a time, from left to right:

(i,j)				
(1,1)	(1,2)	(1,3)	(1,4)	(1,5)
(2,1)	(2,2)	(2,3)	(2,4)	(2,5)
(3,1)	(3,2)	(3,3)	(3,4)	(3,5)
(4,1)	(4,2)	(4,3)	(4,4)	(4,5)
(5,1)	(5,2)	(5,3)	(5,4)	(5,5)

This completes the program for printing a square.

Program 4.2 *Print Square.*

```
/* Prints a square:

    * * * * *
    * * * * *
    * * * * *
    * * * * *
    * * * * *
*/

class square extends basic
{ public static void main(String param[]) throws Exception
  { output out = new output("results");
    out.writeln("Square");
    out.writeln();
    int side = 5;
    for (int i = 1; i <= side; i++)
      { for (int j = 1; j <= side; j++)
          out.write("* ");
        out.writeln();
      }
    out.close();
  }
}
```

4.3   STEPWISE PROGRAMMING

Most people develop programs by a process of trial and error. That is how I do it too (Brinch Hansen 1996):

> I develop a program by writing numerous drafts of the program text. A draft is immediately rejected if it is not in some way simpler and more elegant than the previous one. An improved draft immediately replaces the previous one, which is thrown in the waste basket. Otherwise I would drown in paper and half-baked ideas. As I jump from

one draft to another without slowing myself down, a beautiful design eventually emerges. When that happens, I write a simple description of the program and rewrite it one more time using the same terminology as in the description.

I am referring here to the development of *non-trivial programs*, such as operating systems and compilers.

Edsger Dijkstra (1982) proposed a more systematic programming method, which works well for *small programs* (or small parts of large programs). I will illustrate this method by writing a program that prints a *staircase*:

The essence of the method is that you develop the program in small steps. You start by assuming that the programming language includes a single statement

```
PrintStairs
```

that solves the problem by (unknown) magic.

Most languages do not include such a specialized statement. So, the next step is to define this (non-existing) statement in terms of simpler statements:

```
PrintStairs:
  { int height = 5;
    for (int i = 1; i <= height; i++)
      PrintStep
  }
```

This definition shows that **PrintStairs** is a block that prints five steps. This piece is a mixture of correct Java and another (undefined) statement, called **PrintStep**.

Since we are not dealing with a correct program (yet), I will call this an *abstract program*. It is abstract, because it deliberately ignores certain details I haven't figured out yet. More precisely, it ignores the question of how a single step can be printed.

The third abstract program breaks the process of printing a step into three simpler statements:

```
PrintStep:
  { PrintSpaces
```

```
    PrintAsterisks
    PrintReturn
}
```

Each step is printed as zero or more *spaces* followed by an even number of *asterisks* and a final *return*. It is helpful to draw a more detailed picture of the staircase, which includes *level numbers* of the steps, starting from the top. Here, the spaces have been replaced by digits from 1 to 8:

```
1 12345678**
2 123456****
3 1234******
4 12********
5 **********
```

The following table shows the number of spaces and asterisks for level numbers i from 1 to 5:

level	spaces	asterisks
1	8	2
2	6	4
3	4	6
4	2	8
5	0	10

In general, a staircase of a given `height` has `2*(height−i)` spaces at level `i`. This is what I need to know to program `PrintSpaces`:

```
PrintSpaces:
    for (int j = 1; j <= height - i; j++)
        out.write("  ");
```

Furthermore, there are `2*i` asterisks at level number `i`. So, I have yet another piece of the puzzle:

```
PrintAsterisks:
    for (int j = 1; j <= i; j++)
        out.write("**");
```

The final statement is trivial:

```
PrintReturn:
    out.writeln();
```

At this point, I have broken the program into smaller and smaller pieces, and have reached a level of detail where the simplest pieces are expressed in Java only.

In `PrintStep`, the abstract statements `PrintSpaces`, `PrintAsterisks`, and `PrintReturn` can now be replaced by the corresponding Java statements:

```
PrintStep:
  { for (int j = 1; j <= height - i; j++)
      out.write("  ");
    for (int j = 1; j <= i; j++)
      out.write("**");
    out.writeln();
  }
```

This definition, in turn, replaces `PrintStep` inside the `PrintStairs` piece:

```
PrintStairs:
  { int height = 5;
    for (int i = 1; i <= height; i++)
      { for (int j = 1; j <= height - i; j++)
          out.write("  ");
        for (int j = 1; j <= i; j++)
          out.write("**");
        out.writeln();
      }
  }
```

The remaining details are easy to fill in:

Program 4.3 *Print Stairs.*

```
/* Prints a staircase:

          **
         ****
        ******
       ********
      **********
*/

class stairs extends basic
{ public static void main(String param[]) throws Exception
  { output out = new output();
    out.writeln("Stairs");
    out.writeln();
    int height = 5;
    for (int i = 1; i <= height; i++)
      { for (int j = 1; j <= height - i; j++)
          out.write("  ");
        for (int j = 1; j <= i; j++)
          out.write("**");
        out.writeln();
```

```
        }
    out.writeln(); out.close();
    }
}
```

4.4 PROGRAMMING EXERCISES

Exercise 4.1 Print Chessboard

Write a Java program that prints a chessboard as follows using `for` statements:

Exercise 4.2 Atoms

Here is a list of 14 atoms and the years in which they were discovered:

```
14 atoms and their years of discovery
Argon       1894
Boron       1808
Einsteinium 1952
Fluoride    1886
Hydrogen    1790
Iodine      1811
Nitrogen    1772
Oxygen      1774
Phosphorus  1669
Potassium   1807
Tungsten    1783
Uranium     1789
Vanadium    1830
Yttrium     1794
```

Write a Java program that inputs this list, exactly as shown, from a text file. The program outputs only the atoms that were known in 1808, when John Dalton published the first table of atomic weights. The first few lines of the output are shown below:

```
The following atoms were known by 1808
Boron       1808
Hydrogen    1790
    ...
```

Exercise 4.3 Shakespearean Insults

Write a Java program that outputs 10 random Shakespearean insults, such as:

```
Thou goatish, hasty-witted ratsbane!
Thou loggerheaded, doghearted dewberry!
   ...
Thou churlish, tickle-brained pigeon-egg!
```

Each insult combines one word chosen at random from each of the three columns below:

Column 1	Column 2	Column 3
artless	beetle-headed	barnacle
bootless	clay-brained	coxcomb
churlish	doghearted	dewberry
dissembling	fly-bitten	foot-licker
errant	hasty-witted	gudgeon
fobbing	idle-headed	jolthead
goatish	rough-hewn	lout
impertinent	swag-bellied	minnow
jarring	tickle-brained	pigeon-egg
loggerheaded	weather-bitten	ratsbane

Exercise 4.4 Digital Clock

Write a Java program that behaves like a digital clock. The program displays the following message on the screen:

```
Type day hour min sec am (or pm)
```

If the user types a valid day of the week and time of day, say,

```
Sa 11 59 58 pm
```

the clockwork displays the correct day and time, every second, for the next 100 seconds, say,

```
Sa 11 59 59 pm
Su 12 0 0 am
Su 12 0 1 am
   ...
Su 12 1 38 am
```

The program reports if the user types an invalid day or time.

Exercise 4.5 Rabbits

Write a Java program that computes the number of female rabbits, month by month, under the following assumptions:

1. There are always enough mature males around, so they can be ignored in the computation.

2. At the beginning of the first month there is only one mature female and no immature females.

3. Females mature one month after birth.

4. Each month, every mature female has one female offspring.

5. Females live forever.

Here is the number of females at the end of every month for the first six months:

End of month	Immature females	Mature females	Total females
1	1	1	2
2	1	2	3
3	2	3	5
4	3	5	8
5	5	8	13
6	8	13	21

These numbers illustrate a general rule:

- The number of immature females after n months is equal to the number of mature females after $n - 1$ months.

- The number of mature females after n months is equal to the total number of females after $n - 1$ months.

Your program must compute the number of females, month by month, for 12 months. The program must consist of a main part only. (It may *not* include function definitions, which will be introduced later.)

5

UNBOUNDED REPETITION

This chapter introduces `while` statements for repetition in which the number of iterations required to solve a problem may be unpredictable.

5.1 WHILE STATEMENTS

How many times do you have to toss a coin to get a head? Well, you might get a head the first time. But you might also get 5 tails in a row before you get a head. It is even possible (though highly unlikely) that you will never get a head! The chance of tossing, say, 20 tails in a row is less than one in a million.

Clearly this is a repetitive process where the number of iterations is unknown when the process begins. It is not even known whether the process eventually ends or goes on forever. This is called *unbounded repetition*.

A program that simulates this variant of coin tossing displays the number of tails (if and when the repetition terminates), say,

```
5 tails
```

The program uses a random number to simulate a single `toss`. The number of `tails` is initialized to zero:

```
random toss = new random(1, 2);
int tails = 0;
```

Repeated tossing is expressed by a *while statement*:

```
while (toss.readint() == 2) tails = tails + 1;
```

This structured statement combines a *boolean expression*

```
toss.readint() == 2
```

and a substatement

```
tails = tails + 1;
```

The `while` statement is executed as follows: first, the boolean expression is evaluated by generating a random number `toss.readint()`, which is either 1 or 2:

- If the number is 2, the boolean expression is `true`. In that case, the number of tails is increased by one, by executing the substatement once. Following this, the execution of the `while` statement is repeated.

- If the number is 1, the boolean expression is `false`. This ends the execution of the `while` statement.

In short, the substatement is executed zero or more times, until a random number equal to one is generated.

Program 5.1 *Tails.*

```
/* Simulates coin tosses until a head occurs */

class tails extends basic
{ public static void main(String param[]) throws Exception
  { output out = new output("results");
    random toss = new random(1, 2);
    int tails = 0;
    while (toss.readint() == 2) tails = tails + 1;
    out.writeln(tails + " tails");
    out.close();
  }
}
```

In general, a `while` statement

```
while (B) S
```

denotes zero or more executions of a statement S depending on the evaluation of a boolean expression B. S is called the *body* of the `while` statement.

The `while` statement is executed by following these steps:

1. B is evaluated to obtain a boolean value.

2. There are now two possibilities:

   - If B is `true`, S is executed and, afterwards, steps 1 and 2 are repeated.

   - If B is `false`, the execution of the `while` statement ends.

5.2 MORE STEPWISE PROGRAMMING

A program displays 10 *flash cards*, one at a time, on the screen. Each card asks you to add two random numbers from 1 to 100, for example:

```
What is 37 + 69?
```

If you type an incorrect answer, say,

```
96
```

the program asks you to try to solve the same problem again. This request is repeated until you type the correct answer

```
106
```

The program then acknowledges your answer and displays the next problem.

This example gives me another opportunity to illustrate the method of *stepwise programming*:

1. From an abstract point of view, the whole program can be viewed as a single statement:

```
FlashCards
```

2. My next version splits the program into three smaller pieces:

```
FlashCards:
  { Variables
    Practice
    Terminate
  }
```

3. Using this program, you practice addition by solving, say, n problems:

```
Practice:
  for (i = 1; i <= n; i++)
    NextProblem
```

4. At this point, I begin a list of the variables used:

```
Variables:
  int i, n = 10;
```

So far, I have used a control variable `i` and the number of flash cards `n`. This time, the control variable is declared in the variable list at the beginning of the program (instead of inside the `for` statement). I will say more about this later.

5. After displaying a flash card, the program expects you to solve the problem shown on the card:

```
NextProblem:
  { FlashCard
    SolveProblem
  }
```

6. A card is flashed by generating two random numbers `a` and `b`, and asking you to type the sum of the numbers:

```
FlashCard:
  { a = select.readint();
    b = select.readint();
    out.writeln("What is " + a + " " + " " + b + "?");
  }
```

7. The previous block extends the list of variables with a screen file `out`, a random number generator `select`, two random numbers `a` and `b`, and an upper bound `max`:

```
Variables:
  output out = new output();
  int a, b, i, max = 100, n = 10;
  random select = new random(1, max);
```

8. For each problem, the program insists that you find the correct answer, if necessary by repeated guessing. The program then acknowledges your final (correct) answer:

```
SolveProblem:
  { GuessUntilCorrect
    AcknowledgeAnswer
  }
```

9. The answer you type is input in a variable c. As long as c is *not* equal to the sum a + b, the program asks you to try again and inputs your next guess in the same variable c:

```
GuessUntilCorrect:
  { c = in.readint();
    while (c != a + b)
      { out.writeln("Try again"); c = in.readint(); }
  }
```

Since there is no way of knowing how many attempts you will need to find the right answer, the repeated guessing is defined by a `while` statement.

10. The above block adds a keyboard file in to the list of variables:

```
Variables:
  input in = new input();
  output out = new output();
  int a, b, c, i, max = 100, n = 10;
  random select = new random(1, max);
```

11. The acknowledgment of a correct answer c is straightforward:

```
AcknowledgeAnswer:
  out.writeln(c + " is correct");
```

12. At the end, the program shows that you have solved n problems correctly, and closes the input and output files:

```
Terminate:
  { out.writeln("You have solved " + n
      + " problems correctly!");
    in.close(); out.close(); select.close();
  }
```

By this method of stepwise programming, I have divided the complicated task of developing a complete program into the much simpler tasks of writing 12 small pieces. Roughly half of them are abstract statements; the rest are complete Java statements.

The names of the abstract statements can now gradually be replaced by the corresponding Java statements. This *stepwise substitution of program text* may, for example, be done in the following order:

1. In `SolveProblem`, replace `GuessUntilCorrect` and `Acknowledge-Answer` by the corresponding Java statements.

2. In `NextProblem`, replace `FlashCard` and `SolveProblem` by the equivalent Java blocks.

3. In `Practice`, replace `NextProblem` by its final Java version.

4. In `FlashCards`, replace `Variables`, `Practice`, and `Terminate` by the corresponding Java statements.

By this mechanical transformation, I obtain the following program text:

```
{ input in = new input();
  output out = new output();
  int a, b, c, i, max = 100, n = 10;
  random select = new random(1, max);
  for (i = 1; i <= n; i++)
    { { a = select.readint();
        b = select.readint();
        out.writeln("What is " + a + " + " + b + "?");
      }
      { { c = in.readint();
          while (c != a + b)
            { out.writeln("Try again"); c = in.readint(); }
        }
        out.writeln(c + " is correct");
      }
    }
  { out.writeln("You have solved " + n
      + " problems correctly!");
    in.close(); out.close(); select.close();
  }
}
```

Although this program is correct, it includes eight *superfluous braces*. After removing these braces, I am left with the following **main** block:

```
{ input in = new input();
  output out = new output();
  int a, b, c, i, max = 100, n = 10;
  random select = new random(1, max);
  for (i = 1; i <= n; i++)
    { a = select.readint();
```

```
      b = select.readint();
      out.writeln("What is " + a + " + " + b + "?");
      c = in.readint();
      while (c != a + b)
        { out.writeln("Try again"); c = in.readint(); }
      out.writeln(c + " is correct");
    }
  out.writeln(" You have solved " + n
    + " problems correctly!");
  in.close(); out.close(); select.close();
}
```

In the final program, I have combined variable definitions with the corresponding initial assignments (Program 5.2).

Program 5.2 *Flashcards.*

```
/* Displays 10 flashcards, one at a time, and
   asks the user to add two random numbers
   from 1 to 100. Each problem is repeated
   until the user types the correct answer.
*/

class flashcards extends basic
{ public static void main(String param[]) throws Exception
  { input in = new input();
    output out = new output();
    int n = 10, max = 100;
    random select = new random(1, max);
    for (int i = 1; i <= n; i++)
      { int a = select.readint();
        int b = select.readint();
        out.writeln("What is " + a + " + " + b + "?");
        int c = in.readint();
        while (c != a + b)
          { out.writeln("Try again"); c = in.readint(); }
        out.writeln(c + " is correct");
      }
    out.writeln("You have solved " + n
      + " problems correctly!");
    in.close(); out.close();
  }
}
```

5.3 BLOCKS AND SCOPE

Does it matter *where* variables are declared in a program? To answer that question, I need to clarify the role of *blocks*.

5.3.1   Scope Rules

The purpose of the block concept is to confine the use of a variable to the block in which it is defined. To make this idea precise we need a few rules.

The first rule is necessary to distinguish between different variables defined in the same block:

- *All variables defined in the same block must have different names.*

The block outlined below is meaningless since it introduces two variables named a:

```
{ int a, b, a; ... }
```

The compiler reports the second definition of the ambiguous name a as a variable that is *already defined.*

We must also specify in which part of a block a variable can be used. This part of the block is called the *scope* of the variable. A variable is said to be *known* in its scope.

- *A variable defined in a block is normally known from the end of its definition to the end of the block.*

At this point, I will not explain the only (rare) exception to this rule.

The block skeleton

```
 1 { ...
 2   ...
 3   int max = 10;
     ...
17 }
```

defines a variable max which is *known* from the semicolon in line 3 to the right brace in line 17. The variable cannot be used in lines 1–2, which precede its definition. In this part of the block, the compiler will report the variable as being *undefined.*

Let me repeat the **main** block of the first flash card program with *line numbers*:

```
 1 { input in = new input();
 2   output out = new output();
 3   int a, b, c, i, max = 100, n = 10;
 4   random select = new random(1, max);
 5   for (i = 1; i <= n; i++)
 6     { a = select.readint();
```

```
 7          b = select.readint();
 8          out.writeln("What is " + a + " + " + b + "?");
 9          c = in.readint();
10          while (c != a + b)
11            { out.writeln("Try again"); c = in.readint(); }
12          out.writeln(c + " is correct");
13        }
14    out.writeln("You have solved " + n
15        + "problems correctly!");
16    in.close(); out.close(); select.close();
17 }
```

Since all variables are declared at the beginning of the **main** block, they are (roughly speaking) known in the rest of the block. The following table shows in which lines these variable are *known* and *used*, respectively:

Variable name	Known in lines	Used in lines
a	3–17	6, 8, 10
b	3–17	7–8, 10
c	3–17	9–12
i	3–17	5
in	1–17	1, 9, 11, 16
max	3–17	3–4
out	2–17	2, 8, 11–12, 14–16
n	3–17	3, 5, 14
select	4–17	4, 6–7, 16

The important thing to remember is that each variable can be used only in the lines in which it is known. If that rule is violated, the compiler reports the variable as being *undefined*. This is called a *scope error*.

I remark, in passing, that **in**, **out**, and **select** are considered *variables* of type **input**, **output**, and **random**, respectively. These types are defined by the Java text program.

5.3.2 Nested Scopes

If a block contains another block, say,

```
{ /* outer block */
  ...
  { /* inner block */
    ...
  }
  ...
}
```

the two blocks are said to be *nested*. The smaller block is called an *inner block* of the larger block. The latter, in turn, is called an *outer block* of the smaller one.

In the previous program, the body of the `for` statement is an inner block of the main block.

A variable is said to be *local* to the block in which it is defined. If the scope of a variable includes an inner block that uses the variable, then the variable is said to be *global* to the inner block.

In the final flash card program, the variable `max` is local to the `main` block and global to the body of the `for` statement.

When all variables are declared at the beginning of the `main` block, they are potentially accessible throughout the program. In most cases, this is logically unnecessary and therefore confusing to someone who tries to understand the program.

An alternative method is to *define variables inside the smallest blocks that use them*. This design principle clarifies the logical relationship between variables and statements. In a later chapter, you will see that this is also the essence of object-oriented programming.

In the second version of the previous example, some of the variables are now declared in the `main` block of the program, while others are declared in the body of the `for` statement:

```
 1 { input in = new input();
 2   output out = new output();
 3   int max = 100, n = 10;
 4   random select = new random(1, max);
 5   for (int i = 1; i <= n; i++)
 6     { int a = select.readint();
 7       int b = select.readint();
 8       out.writeln("What is " + a + " + " + b + "?");
 9       int c = in.readint();
10       while (c != a + b)
11         { out.writeln("Try again"); c = in.readint(); }
12       out.writeln(c + " is correct");
13     }
14   out.writeln("You have solved " + n
15     + "problems correctly!");
16   in.close(); out.close(); select.close();
17 }
```

However, the previous *scope rule* still applies: every variable must be defined before it can be used, and each definition is valid only to the end of the block that introduces the variable (see the table below).

Variable name	Known in lines	Used in lines
a	6–13	6, 8, 10
b	7–13	7–8, 10
c	9–13	9–12
i	5–13	5
in	1–17	1, 9, 11, 16
max	3–17	3–4
out	2–17	2, 8, 11–12, 14–16
n	3–17	3, 5, 14
select	4–17	4, 6–7, 16

You may wonder if it is possible to define two variables with the *same name* in *different blocks*. We will cross that bridge when we come to it.

5.3.3   Final Remarks

At first sight, you may find the scope rules of programming languages complicated. In reality, however, blocks and scopes are *thinking tools* that help you divide complex problems into simpler problems that can be solved one at a time. It doesn't matter whether you are talking about computer programming, engineering, architecture, sculpture, literature, music, or mathematics: *divide and conquer* is the essence of problem solving in all fields of human endeavor. It is the way we think about complex problems.

5.4   FOR STATEMENTS REVISITED

A `for` statement of the form

```
for (int i = e; i <= f; i++) S
```

defines a control variable `i`, two expressions, `e` and `f`, and a body `S`. The scope of the control variable extends from the first semicolon to the end of the body `S`.

This `for` statement has the same effect as the following block:

```
{ int i = e;
  while (i <= f)
    { S; i = i + 1; }
}
```

From this block, you can draw the following conclusions:

- The control variable is local to the `for` statement and global to its body. So, the control variable is *undefined* before and after the `for` statement.

- Whereas the lower bound `e` is only evaluated once, the upper bound `f` is reevaluated for every iteration.

From now on, I will call a `for` statement a *for block* if it defines a local control variable.

I have described only the simplest form of Java's `for` statement. This is the only kind I will use in this book. I don't think it helps anybody to study unnecessary complexity in Java (or any other programming language).

5.5   PROGRAMMING EXERCISES

Exercise 5.1   Russian Roulette

Russian roulette is a deadly game of chance in which you spin the cylinder of a six-shooter holding only one bullet, point the gun at your head, and pull the trigger.

Write a Java program that plays this game. Use a random number generator to select the chamber in which the bullet is inserted. Then select chambers at random and check if you fired the bullet.

If you play the game 10 times without firing the bullet, you win and the program displays the following lines:

```
 1: click!
 2: click!
 3: click!
 4: click!
 5: click!
 6: click!
 7: click!
 8: click!
 9: click!
10: click!
YOU WIN!
```

If you fire the bullet after, say, three clicks, you lose and the output is:

```
 1: click!
 2: click!
 3: click!
BANG!
```

Exercise 5.2 The Game of Craps

In craps you roll two dice:

1. If the first roll is a 7 or 11, you win.

2. If the first roll is a 2, 3, or 12, you lose.

3. If the first roll is a 4, 5, 6, 8, 9, or 10, you keep on rolling the dice until you either

   - win by repeating the first number you rolled (you "make your point"), or

   - lose by rolling a 7 (you "crap out").

Write a Java program that uses two random number generators (one for each die) to play a single game of craps until the game is either won or lost. The program displays the result of each throw of the dice and the final outcome of the game. Here is the output of four different games played by the program:

```
You got 11 and won!
You got 3 and lost!
You got 8, 11, 12, 4, 8 and made your point!
You got 5, 9, 8, 7 and crapped out!
```

Exercise 5.3 The Game of Nim

Write a Java program that plays Nim. You and the program take turns removing 1, 2, or 3 coins from a pile of 20 coins. Whoever is forced to remove the last coin loses. You type the number of coins you want to remove. The number of coins removed by the program is a random number from 1 to 3.

Here is an example of the output displayed on the screen during a game:

```
20 coins left. How many do you want to remove?
You removed 3. I removed 1.
16 coins left. How many do you want to remove?
You removed 2. I removed 2.
12 coins left. How many do you want to remove?
You removed 1. I removed 2.
9 coins left. How many do you want to remove?
You cannot remove 8. Try again.
You removed 3. I removed 2.
4 coins left. How many do you want to remove?
You removed 1. I removed 3.
I lost!
```

Exercise 5.4 The Typing Monkey

Write a Java program that asks you to type a three-letter word (using small letters only). For example:

```
Type a three-letter word
dog
```

The program then simulates a monkey that types three random letters at a time until it eventually types the selected word, say,

```
"dog" typed after 27772 attempts
```

(The program does not output any other words typed by the monkey.)

Hint: use random numbers and switch statements to assign random letters to three character variables a, b, and c. Then generate a three-letter word by extending an empty string "" with the random characters:

```
String typed = "" + a + b + c;
```

Exercise 5.5 Roulette

Write a Java program that plays the game of Roulette. The game is played by spinning a wheel with a small ball and waiting until the ball at random ends up in one of 38 holes.

You enter the casino with $1000. The first time the wheel spins you select the winning number as your lucky number. Then you bet $1 on your lucky number and watch the wheel spin again: If you win, the bank pays you $35; otherwise, you lose your bet. You continue to bet $1 on your lucky number until you have lost all your money.

The program displays the number of times you won and lost. It also shows the largest amount of money you had at any time during the game, say,

```
You lost 3030 times, and won 58 times.
At one point, you had $1055.
```

6

TEXT FILES

A *data structure* is a group of related data items that are regarded as a single entity. A *text file* is a data structure that provides *sequential access* to characters and strings. This chapter explains how text files are stored and processed on a computer.

6.1 SEQUENTIAL FILES

When my son Thomas was eight years old he wrote this poem:

```
THE BRAIN

The brain helps to move your legs,
hands, and toes.
The brain helps us do many things.
It is good to have a brain.
```

Suppose the poem is stored as a text file named `poem`. What is the structure of this text file? Well, let me first mention that a text file includes characters that are invisible on printed paper (and screens). The *invisible characters* are the space and newline characters, named `sp` and `nl`. There is also an invisible character, named `eof`, that marks the end of the file.

To show *where* these characters occur, I will reprint the poem in a slightly different form:

```
THE␣BRAIN◁
◁
The␣brain␣helps␣to␣move␣your␣legs,◁
hands,␣and␣toes.◁
The␣brain␣helps␣us␣do␣many␣things.◁
It␣is␣good␣to␣have␣a␣brain.◁
⊙
```

This time I have used *pictorial signs* to represent the invisible characters. These signs are *not* part of the file; they are used only to illustrate the file structure:

Character name	Pictorial sign
sp	␣
nl	◁
eof	⊙

On a printer (or screen), the poem appears as a two-dimensional text of six lines. However, the computer treats a newline character like any other character and stores the text file as a one-dimensional *sequence of characters*:

```
THE␣BRAIN◁ ... ◁It␣is␣good␣to␣have␣a␣brain.◁⊙
```

Since text files can only be input and output one character at a time, they are called *sequential files*.

6.2 READING A FILE

The file system of a computer is similar to a collection of prerecorded cassette tapes. Each cassette tape holds a single text file. Opening an input file is analogous to selecting a cassette, inserting it in a tape player, and rewinding the tape. The file can now be read by moving the tape across a read head. At the end of the tape, the file is closed by removing the cassette from the player and putting it back in the collection of recorded tapes.

Since a file is not really a tape that moves across a read head, I prefer to describe it in slightly different terms:

The opening of an input file creates a device that can read the file, character by character, from the beginning. This device uses a hidden variable, called the *file pointer*, to define the position of the next input character within the file. When a program reads the file, *the file pointer conceptually moves across the text* in discrete steps. Since this input device is implemented by software (rather than hardware), it is an *abstract device*.

The statement

```
input in = new input("poem");
```

opens an existing text file, named `poem`, for input and positions the file pointer at the first character in the file:

```
| THE⊔BRAIN◁ ... ◁It⊔is⊔good⊔to⊔have⊔a⊔brain.◁⊙ |
  ↑
```

In this picture, the file text is framed to illustrate the similarity of files and tapes. The file pointer is shown as an arrow ↑ below the framed text.

The statement

```
char ch = in.read();
```

reads the first input character T into a variable `ch` and moves the file pointer to the second character H:

```
| THE⊔BRAIN◁ ... ◁It⊔is⊔good⊔to⊔have⊔a⊔brain.◁⊙ |
  ↑
```

The variable `ch` now holds a copy of the first character. Consequently, the condition `ch == 'T'` is `true`.

When the program executes another input statement

```
ch = in.read();
```

the second character H is read into the same variable `ch`. Since this assignment overwrites the previous value of `ch`, we now have `ch == 'H'`. At the same time, the file pointer has advanced to the third character E:

```
| THE⊔BRAIN◁ ... ◁It⊔is⊔good⊔to⊔have⊔a⊔brain.◁⊙ |
   ↑
```

When the program has read nine characters, the file pointer is at the first newline character:

```
| THE⊔BRAIN◁ ... ◁It⊔is⊔good⊔to⊔have⊔a⊔brain.◁⊙ |
    ↑
```

The next read operation inputs the newline character and makes `ch ==` `nl`.

When the program has input the whole poem, the file pointer has reached the end of file character:

```
THE␣BRAIN◁ ... ◁It␣is␣good␣to␣have␣a␣brain.◁⊙
                                              ↑
```

After the next read operation, the assertion `ch == eof` is `true`. Since further input is impossible, the file should now be closed:

```
in.close();
```

It should now be obvious that a program can read a file as follows (without doing anything with the characters):

```
{ input in = new input("poem");
  char ch = in.read();
  while (ch != eof) ch = in.read();
  in.close();
}
```

There are two ways to obtain the next input character:

- The function call `in.read()` returns the next input character, *and* moves the file pointer one character ahead.

- The function call `in.next()` returns the next input character, *without* advancing the file pointer.

If a program calls `next` followed by `read`, the next input character is returned twice before the file pointer is advanced. This insight can be used to shorten the input block:

```
{ input in = new input("poem");
  while (in.next() != eof) char ch = in.read();
  in.close();
}
```

The function call

```
in.more()
```

yields the same value as the boolean expression

```
in.next() != eof
```

In other words, `in.more()` is `true`, if there is *more input* to be read from the file; otherwise, it is `false`.

Consequently, we can *scan* a file by means of a single `while` statement:

```
{ input in = new input("poem");
  while (in.more()) char ch = in.read();
  in.close();
}
```

6.3 WRITING A FILE

Opening an output file is analogous to inserting a blank cassette tape in a tape recorder, and rewinding the tape. The tape can now be recorded by moving the tape across a write head. At the end of the recording, the file is closed by removing the cassette from the recorder and adding it to the collection of recorded tapes.

In slightly different words, the opening of an output file creates an abstract device that can write a new file, character by character, from the beginning. This device uses a *file pointer* to define the position of the next output character within the file.

Let me explain how the same poem can be output in a new file.

The statement

```
output out = new output("results");
```

opens an empty file, named `results`, for output and positions the file pointer at the beginning of the file:

The statement

```
out.write('T');
```

outputs the first character T to the file, and moves the file pointer to the next empty position:

```
┌─────────────────────────────────────────┐
│ T                                        │
└─────────────────────────────────────────┘
  ↑
```

When the program executes another output statement

```
out.write('H');
```

the file is extended with the second character H, and the file pointer is again
advanced by one position:

TH

↑

When the program has written nine characters, the file pointer marks
the position of the first newline character (to be output next):

THE␣BRAIN

      ↑

When the program has output the whole poem, the file pointer has
reached its final position where an end of file character will be output:

THE␣BRAIN◁ ... ◁It␣is␣good␣to␣have␣a␣brain.◁

                                        ↑

The statement

```
out.close();
```

completes the file by outputting an end of file character:

THE␣BRAIN◁ ... ◁It␣is␣good␣to␣have␣a␣brain.◁⊙

The file is now closed for further output.

6.4   COPYING A FILE

A file is rarely output as a sequence of characters defined in the program
text. In practice, an output file is often the result of processing one or more
input files. The simplest example is Program 6.1, which makes a copy of an
existing file.

Program 6.1 *Copying a File.*

```
/* Makes a copy of an existing file. */

class copy extends basic
{ public static void main(String param[]) throws Exception
  { input in = new input("poem");
    output out = new output("results");
    while (in.more())
      { char ch = in.read(); out.write(ch); }
    in.close(); out.close();
  }
}
```

6.5 DATA EXTRACTION

A common data processing problem is to examine data items and choose those that meet some criterion. A trivial example of *data extraction* is a program that scans the previous poem and prints *consonants only*. More precisely, the program skips all vowels and copies the rest of the text:

```
TH BRN

Th brn hlps t mv r lgs,
hnds, nd ts.
Th brn hlps s d mn thngs.
t s gd t hv  brn.
```

This example shows that consonants convey much more information than vowels, perhaps because the English alphabet has 20 consonants, but only 6 vowels.

The program must distinguish between three kinds of characters: *consonants*, *vowels*, and *non-letters*. If the program uses a straightforward switch statement for this purpose, there are 53 cases. Fortunately, *the switch statement allows you to group related cases together:*

```
switch (ch)
  { case 'b': case 'c': case 'd': case 'f': case 'g': case 'h':
    case 'j': case 'k': case 'l': case 'm': case 'n': case 'p':
    case 'q': case 'r': case 's': case 't': case 'v': case 'w':
    case 'x': case 'z':
    case 'B': case 'C': case 'D': case 'F': case 'G': case 'H':
    case 'J': case 'K': case 'L': case 'M': case 'N': case 'P':
    case 'Q': case 'R': case 'S': case 'T': case 'V': case 'W':
    case 'X': case 'Z':
      /* consonant */ out.write(ch); break;
    case 'a': case 'e': case 'i': case 'o': case 'u': case 'y':
```

```
      case 'A': case 'E': case 'I': case 'O': case 'U': case 'Y':
        /* vowel */ ; break;
      default:
        /* non-letter */ out.write(ch); break;
  }
```

However, it is simpler just to distinguish between vowels, which must be skipped, and all other characters, which must be copied. This reduces the number of cases to 13:

```
switch (ch)
  { case 'a': case 'e': case 'i': case 'o': case 'u': case 'y':
    case 'A': case 'E': case 'I': case 'O': case 'U': case 'Y':
      /* vowel */ ; break;
    default:
      /* non-vowel */ out.write(ch); break;
  }
```

My own preference for this problem is the following if statement:

```
if
 ((ch != 'a') & (ch != 'A') &
  (ch != 'e') & (ch != 'E') &
  (ch != 'i') & (ch != 'I') &
  (ch != 'o') & (ch != 'O') &
  (ch != 'u') & (ch != 'U') &
  (ch != 'y') & (ch != 'Y'))
    /* non-vowel */ out.write(ch);
```

If you feel that the choice between these solutions is a matter of personal taste, then you already appreciate that *programming is an aesthetic discipline guided by sound principles and a sense of elegance.* In that respect, computing is no different than any other intellectual discipline (Wechsler 1978).

The complete program for printing consonants is shown below:

Program 6.2 *Print Consonants.*

```
/* Reads text, skips all vowels and prints the rest. */

class consonants extends basic
 { public static void main(String param[]) throws Exception
   { input in = new input("poem");
     output out = new output("results");
     while (in.more())
       { char ch = in.read();
         if
           ((ch != 'a') & (ch != 'A') &
            (ch != 'e') & (ch != 'E') &
```

```
                (ch != 'i') & (ch != 'I') &
                (ch != 'o') & (ch != 'O') &
                (ch != 'u') & (ch != 'U') &
                (ch != 'y') & (ch != 'Y'))
                  /* non-vowel */ out.write(ch);
        }
      in.close(); out.close();
    }
  }
```

6.6 DATA CONVERSION

Let me print the same poem again in *full capitals*:

```
THE BRAIN

THE BRAIN HELPS TO MOVE YOUR LEGS,
HANDS, AND TOES.
THE BRAIN HELPS US DO MANY THINGS.
IT IS GOOD TO HAVE A BRAIN.
```

The small letters are now replaced by the corresponding capital letters. This is an example of *data conversion*.

You can, of course, program this conversion the hard way by means of a `switch` statement with a separate case for every small letter. But this time I want to show you another method, which is based on the numeric representation of characters inside the computer.

6.6.1 Character Numbers

The character set used by most American computers is called *ASCII* (The American Standard Code for Information Interchange). In a computer memory, each character is represented by an integer from 0 to 127. These integers are called *character numbers* or *ordinal numbers*.

Table 6.1 shows the ASCII characters and their ordinal values. Characters 0 to 31 and 127 are (invisible) control characters (which include the newline character `nl`). For the data conversion problem, we only need to know the ordinal values of the *letters*.

Table 6.1 *The ASCII Characters.*

0	nul	32	sp	64	@	96	`
1	soh	33	!	65	A	97	a
2	stx	34	"	66	B	98	b
3	etx	35	#	67	C	99	c
4	eot	36	$	68	D	100	d
5	enq	37	%	69	E	101	e
6	ack	38	&	70	F	102	f
7	bel	39	´	71	G	103	g
8	bs	40	(	72	H	104	h
9	ht	41	)	73	I	105	i
10	nl	42	*	74	J	106	j
11	vt	43	+	75	K	107	k
12	ff	44	,	76	L	108	l
13	cr	45	-	77	M	109	m
14	so	46	.	78	N	110	n
15	si	47	/	79	O	111	o
16	dle	48	0	80	P	112	p
17	dc1	49	1	81	Q	113	q
18	dc2	50	2	82	R	114	r
19	dc3	51	3	83	S	115	s
20	dc4	52	4	84	T	116	t
21	nak	53	5	85	U	117	u
22	syn	54	6	86	V	118	v
23	etb	55	7	87	W	119	w
24	can	56	8	88	X	120	x
25	em	57	9	89	Y	121	y
26	sub	58	:	90	Z	122	z
27	esc	59	;	91	[	123	{
28	fs	60	<	92	\	124		
29	gs	61	=	93	]	125	}
30	rs	62	>	94	^	126	~
31	us	63	?	95	_	127	del

6.6.2   Type Conversion

The value of the expression

    (int)ch

is the ordinal number of the character ch.

Example: `(int)'e' == 101`

The value of the expression

`(char)n`

is the character with the ordinal number n.

Example: `(char)69 == 'E'`

These expressions define *type conversions*:

- The `(int)` operator converts a character value to an integer value.

- The `(char)` operator converts an integer value to a character value.

If you start with any small letter in Table 6.1 and count 32 characters backwards, you will find the corresponding capital letter. For example, the letters e and E are characters number 101 and 69, respectively.

In other words, if ch is a small letter, the corresponding capital letter must be character number

`(int)ch - 32`

When an arithmetic expression is evaluated, a character operand ch is automatically converted to its ordinal number. So, the above expression can be reduced to:

`ch - 32`

The constant 32 is the distance in Table 6.1 between any small letter and the corresponding capital letter, for example:

`'a' - 'A' == 32`

Consequently, the expression ch - 32 can be rewritten as

`ch - 'a' + 'A'`

(I will explain shortly why this is a good idea.)

This expression defines the ordinal number of a capital letter. The capital letter itself is obtained by converting its ordinal number to a character:

`(char)(ch - 'a' + 'A')`

In the data conversion program, the following if statement replaces any
small letter by the corresponding capital letter and leaves any other character
unchanged:

```
if (('a' <= ch) & (ch <= 'z'))
  out.write((char)(ch - 'a' + 'A'));
else out.write(ch);
```

6.6.3   The Program "Full Capitalization"

Program 6.3 *Full Capitalization.*

```
/* Replaces small letters in a text file
   by the corresponding capital letters.
*/

class capitals extends basic
{ public static void main(String param[]) throws Exception
  { input in = new input("poem");
    output out = new output("results");
    while (in.more())
      { char ch = in.read();
        if (('a' <= ch) & (ch <= 'z'))
          out.write((char)(ch - 'a' + 'A'));
        else out.write(ch);
      }
    in.close(); out.close();
  }
}
```

Since I replaced the character distance 32 by 'a' - 'A', this program
does *not* depend on the ASCII character numbers in Table 6.1. Instead, the
conversion program makes a much weaker assumption about the available
character set (which need not be ASCII):

- The capital letters are ordered alphabetically with consecutive ordinal
  numbers.

- The small letters are ordered alphabetically with consecutive ordinal
  numbers.

It is a sound design principle to *make as few assumptions as possible.* If
you introduce additional (unnecessary) assumptions, your programs will be
more difficult to understand and modify.

6.7 SYNTAX-DIRECTED PROGRAMMING

The next programming problem is formulated as an exercise (for me). You may wish to skip this section on a first reading, but of course, I hope you won't.

6.7.1 A Readability Test

Write a Java program that reads a text file and evaluates its readability based on the average sentence length in words:

4th grade	8 or less
5th grade	9 to 11
6th grade	12 to 14
7–8th grade	15 to 17
High school	18 to 24
College	25 and up

The text consists of one or more sentences. Each sentence consists of one or more words separated by commas, spaces, or newline characters. A sentence ends with a colon, question mark, or period. After scanning the text, the program displays a message, such as,

```
6th grade level: 13 words per sentence.
```

Test the program with the following input text files (Flesch 1962):

> Learning a language need not be dull, if we fortify our efforts by scientific curiosity about the relative defects and merits of the language we are studying, about its relation to other languages which people speak, and about the social agencies which have affected its growth or about circumstances which have molded its character in the course of history.

> Learning a language need not be dull. We can fortify our efforts by scientific curiosity about the language we are studying: What are its relative defects and merits? How is it related to other languages people speak? What social agencies have affected its growth? What circumstances have molded its character in the course of history?

6.7.2 Syntax Description of Text

The program must be able to analyze *any* file that fits the previous description:

"The text consists of one or more sentences. Each sentence consists of one or more words separated by commas, spaces, or newline characters. A sentence ends with a colon, question mark, or period."

What I am describing here is the correct order in which words, punctuation marks, and other characters can occur in sentences. I am, in other words, describing the *syntax* of the text.

When you are writing a program for text processing, a precise definition of the input syntax is essential. Otherwise, you will only have a rough idea of what the program is supposed to do. If the text has a simple structure, you may be able to describe its syntax in natural language. But, for more complicated problems, you will need a formal definition of syntax.

This is particularly true if you are developing a *compiler* that inputs a program text and outputs executable code. It is not practical to define the syntax of all possible Java programs in English. The *grammar* of a programming language is a collection of rules that define the complete syntax of the language. The introduction of *Backus–Naur notation* for *syntax rules* was a major breakthrough in programming (Naur 1992).

Syntax rules can be used to guide the design of any program that analyzes text. I will begin the development of the readability test by defining the syntax of all possible input texts. The *input grammar* consists of five syntax rules:

```
1.  Text:
        Sentence { Sentence } EOF
2.  Sentence:
        Word { AnotherWord } EOS
3.  Word:
        Letter { Letter }
4.  AnotherWord:
        [ , ] Word
5.  EOS:
        : | ? | .
```

These rules can be read as follows:

1. A Text consists of one or more sentences followed by an end of file character EOF. The notation { Sentence } means "zero or more sentences."

   Examples: (See the input files in the problem definition.)

2. A Sentence consists of one or more words followed by an end of sentence character EOS.

Example: He who cannot write, can surely review.

3. A Word consists of one or more Letter(s).

   Examples: a   How

4. The term AnotherWord refers to a word that may be preceded by a comma. The notation [,] means "one comma or none."

   Examples: be   , dull

5. An *end of sentence* character EOS is either a colon, a question mark, or a period. The choice is expressed by a vertical bar | that can be pronounced "or."

   Examples: :   ?   .

6.7.3   Tokens

A text defined by this grammar is a sequence of symbols called *tokens*:

```
Token:
  Word | , | : | ? | . | EOF
```

Any Token may be preceded and followed by one or more blanks. A Blank is either a *space* or a *newline* character.

The program will

- skip blanks (if any) before the *first* token;

- skip blanks (if any) after *each* token.

6.7.4   Parsing the Text

I will use the previous grammar to illustrate a form of stepwise programming in which the program structure is guided by the input syntax.

The initial aim is to write a program that inputs a text without doing anything with it. (Later, I will add the missing details.) Such a program is called a *parser* (from the word "parse" which means "to describe a series of words grammatically").

To simplify matters, I will assume that the input text is syntactically correct. If you are interesting in learning about systematic methods for dealing with *syntax errors*, you should study compiler design (Brinch Hansen 1985).

The basic idea of *syntax-directed programming* is simple:

- *For each syntax rule, write an abstract statement with the same name.*

You can write the program pieces in any order you like. We might as well start with the syntax rule that defines a complete `Text`:

```
Text:
  { in.readblanks();
      ...
  }
```

The input statement skips initial blanks (if any).

I don't know yet how to parse a `Sentence`. But I know that the syntax of a sentence is defined by another rule. So, eventually I will have to program an abstract statement, named `Sentence`. At this early stage of the program development, I will just use the name of this (unknown) statement to denote the parsing of the first sentence:

```
Text:
  { in.readblanks();
    Sentence
      ...
  }
```

- *To parse a text described by a syntax rule, use an abstract statement with the same name as the rule.*

- *Later, replace the abstract statement by the corresponding Java statements.*

The syntax notation { `Sentence` } stands for zero or more `Sentence`(s). Since the number of sentences is not known beforehand, the program must use *unbounded repetition* to parse these sentences (if any). The repetition stops when the program reaches the *end of file* character `EOF`:

```
Text:
  { in.readblanks();
    Sentence
    while (in.more())
      Sentence
  }
```

- *Use a* while *statement to parse zero or more occurrences of the same text element.*

Since a while statement can parse *zero or more* Sentence(s), it can certainly also handle *one or more* Sentence(s). Consequently, I can omit the first Sentence statement and just write:

```
Text:
  { in.readblanks();
    while (in.more())
      Sentence
  }
```

I assume that the text conforms to its grammar. According to syntax rule 1, a text consists of at least one Sentence. It may, nevertheless, be helpful to write this assumption in the program and stop the execution if it isn't satisfied:

```
Text:
  { in.readblanks();
    assume(in.more(), "empty text");
    while (in.more())
      Sentence
  }
```

The program parses a Sentence by means of three abstract statements and an abstract expression (to be defined later):

```
Sentence:
  { Word
    while (NotEOS)
      AnotherWord
    EndMark
  }
```

Within a Sentence, the parsing of separate words continues as long as the next character is *not* an *end of sentence* character EOS. In other words, the repetition is controlled by the boolean expression:

```
NotEOS:
  (in.next() != ':') & (in.next() != '?')
    & (in.next() != '.')
```

A Word is parsed by reading it into a string variable, and skipping trailing blanks (if any):

```
Word:
  { String word = in.readname();
    in.readblanks();
  }
```

If `AnotherWord` begins with a comma, the program skips the comma (and any blanks after it). The program then reads the `Word` and skips trailing blanks (if any):

```
AnotherWord:
  { if (in.next() == ',')
      { in.readnext(); in.readblanks(); }
    word = in.readname(); in.readblanks();
  }
```

- *Use an* if *statement to parse zero or one occurrence of a text element.*

An *end of sentence* character `EOS` is skipped as follows:

```
EOS:
  { in.readnext(); in.readblanks(); }
```

The final step is to replace abstract statements and expressions by Java text. After eliminating superfluous braces, I obtain:

```
Text:
  { in.readblanks();
    assume(in.more(), "empty text");
    while (in.more())
      { String word = in.readname();
        in.readblanks();
        while ((in.next() != ':') & (in.next() != '?')
          & (in.next() !='.'))
            { if (in.next() == ',')
                { in.readnext(); in.readblanks(); }
              word = in.readname();
              in.readblanks();
            }
        in.readnext(); in.readblanks();
      }
  }
```

6.7.5   The Program "Readability Test"

Program 6.4 includes variables and statements that count the number of sentences and words and compute the readability score of the input text. The input grammar has been added as a program comment.

Program 6.4 *Readability Test.*

```
/* Reads an English text and computes a readability
   score based on the average sentence length in words.

   Text:
     { Sentence } EOF
   Sentence:
     Word { AnotherWord } EOS
   Word:
     Letter { Letter }
   AnotherWord:
     [ , ] Word
   EOS:
     : | ? | .
*/

class readability extends basic
{ public static void main(String param[]) throws Exception
  { input keyboard = new input();
    output screen = new output();
    screen.writeln("Type file name");
    input in = new input(keyboard.readword());
    output out = new output("results");
    in.readblanks();
    assume(in.more(), "empty text");
    int sentences = 0, words = 0;
    while (in.more())
      { String word = in.readname();
        in.readblanks();
        words = words + 1;
        while ((in.next() != ':') & (in.next() != '?')
          & (in.next() != '.'))
            { if (in.next() == ',')
                { in.readnext(); in.readblanks(); }
              word = in.readname();
              in.readblanks();
              words = words + 1;
            }
        in.readnext(); in.readblanks();
        sentences = sentences + 1;
      }
    int length = words/sentences;
    if (length <= 8) out.write("4th grade");
    else if (length <= 11) out.write("5th grade");
    else if (length <= 14) out.write("6th grade");
    else if (length <= 17) out.write("7-8th grade");
    else if (length <= 24) out.write("High school");
    else out.write("College");
    out.writeln(" level: " + length
      + " words per sentence");
```

```
      in.close(); out.close();
      keyboard.close(); screen.close();
  }
}
```

When this program analyzes the first text file, it computes a high (un)readability score:

```
College level:  59 words per sentence
```

The second text file is found to be at the

```
5th grade level:  9 words per sentence
```

6.8   PROGRAMMING EXERCISES

Exercise 6.1   Encode Message

Write a Java program that inputs a text file in capital letters, say,

```
ONCE UPON A TIME AND A VERY GOOD TIME IT
WAS THERE WAS A MOOCOW COMING DOWN ALONG
THE ROAD AND THIS MOOCOW THAT WAS COMING
DOWN ALONG THE ROAD MET A NICENS LITTLE
BOY NAMED BABY TUCKOO
   A PORTRAIT OF THE ARTIST AS A YOUNG MAN
   BY JAMES JOYCE
```

and outputs a corresponding *encoded message*. Spaces and newline characters are just copied. Each input letter is replaced by the corresponding output letter shown below:

```
Input letter:  ABCDEFGHIJKLMNOPQRSTUVWXYZ
Output letter: TUVWXYZABCDEFGHIJKLMNOPQRS
```

Use the above example as a test case.

Exercise 6.2   Decode Message

Write a Java program that inputs a text file in capital letters, say,

```
HGVX NIHG T MBFX TGW T OXKR ZHHW MBFX BM
PTL MAXKX PTL T FHHVHP VHFBGZ WHPG TEHGZ
MAX KHTW TGW MABL FHHVHP MATM PTL VHFBGZ
WHPG TEHGZ MAX KHTW FXM T GBVXGL EBMMEX
UHR GTFXW UTUR MNVDHH
   T IHKMKTBM HY MAX TKMBLM TL T RHNGZ FTG
   UR CTFXL CHRVX
```

and outputs a corresponding *decoded message*. Spaces and newline characters are just copied. Each input letter is replaced by the corresponding output letter shown below:

```
Input letter:  ABCDEFGHIJKLMNOPQRSTUVWXYZ
Output letter: HIJKLMNOPQRSTUVWXYZABCDEFG
```

Use the above example as a test case.

Exercise 6.3 Morse Code

Write a Java program that inputs a text file in capital letters and outputs the corresponding Morse code:

```
A  .-      G  --.     M  --      S  ...     Y  -.--
B  -...    H  ....    N  -.      T  -       Z  --..
C  -.-.    I  ..      O  ---     U  ..-
D  -..     J  .---    P  .--.    V  ...-
E  .       K  -.-     Q  --.-    W  .--
F  ..-.    L  .-..    R  .-.     X  -..-
```

Use the following input text to test the program:

```
THE QUICK BROWN FOX JUMPS OVER THE LAZY DOG
```

Skip spaces in the input, and output each letter and its Morse code on a separate line:

```
T  -
H  ....
E  .
Q  --.-
   etc.
G  --.
```

Exercise 6.4 Print Text

Write a Java program that inputs a text file and outputs it with line numbers. The input consists of zero or more lines followed by an end of file character. A line consists of zero or more graphic characters followed by a newline character. A graphic character is either a letter, a digit, a special character, or a space. In more formal terms, the input syntax is defined by the following syntax rules:

```
Input:
  { Line } EOF
Line:
  { GraphicCharacter } NL
GraphicCharacter:
  Letter | Digit | SpecialCharacter | Space
```

In the output, each line consists of a line number with three character positions followed by a space and the corresponding input line (*Hint:* see 1.6.3). Use the program to output Program 6.1 as follows:

```
 1 /* Makes a copy of an existing file. */
 2
 3 class copy extends basic
 4 { public static void main(String param[]) throws Exception
 5   { input in = new input("poem");
 6     output out = new output("results");
 7     while (in.more())
 8       { char ch = in.read(); out.write(ch); }
 9     in.close(); out.close();
10   }
11 }
```

Exercise 6.5 Jazz Records

Write a Java program that inputs a list of the ratings and titles of jazz records and
outputs the titles of the ones that have a four-star rating. Use the program to input
the following record list (Cook 1994):

> **** Birth Of The Cool
> ** Miles Davis With Horns
> *** Dig
> **** Milestones
> **** Cookin' At The Plugged Nickel
> *** No Blues
> **** In A Silent Way

and output the following selection

> Birth Of The Cool
> Milestones
> Cookin' At The Plugged Nickel
> In A Silent Way

In general, the input consists of zero or more records followed by an end of file character. Each record consists of a rating followed by a title and a newline character:

```
Input:
  { Record } EOF
Record:
  Rating Title NL
Rating:
  * | ** | *** | ****
Title:
  GraphicCharacter { GraphicCharacter }
```

Every rating and title may be preceded and followed by blanks.

SIMPLE ARRAYS

This chapter introduces the *array*, a data structure that provides *direct access* to a group of variables of the same type.

7.1 THE PURPOSE OF ARRAYS

A hotel uses a computer to keep track of free and occupied rooms. If you try to write a program for this problem, you will soon discover that we need another programming concept.

7.1.1 The Limitations of Simple Variables

Let's say the hotel only has 10 rooms. The first idea that comes to mind is to use a separate boolean variable for each room to indicate whether or not the room is free:

```
boolean
  free1 = true, free2 = true, free3 = true, free4 = true,
  free5 = true, free6 = true, free7 = true, free8 = true,
  free9 = true, free10 = true;
```

Initially, all rooms are free (as shown above). After a while, some rooms may be free, while others are occupied. The following if statements output a list of all free rooms (if any):

```
if (free1) out.writeln("Room 1 is free");
if (free2) out.writeln("Room 2 is free");
```

```
if (free3) out.writeln("Room 3 is free");
if (free4) out.writeln("Room 4 is free");
if (free5) out.writeln("Room 5 is free");
if (free6) out.writeln("Room 6 is free");
if (free7) out.writeln("Room 7 is free");
if (free8) out.writeln("Room 8 is free");
if (free9) out.writeln("Room 9 is free");
if (free10) out.writeln("Room 10 is free");
```

To determine, for example, if room number 3 is free, it is necessary to test the value of the corresponding variable `free3`. Since each test examines a different variable, we end up with 10 trivial variants of the same `if` statement. This may be tolerable if there are no more than 10 replicas of the same statement. But it is clearly impractical for a hotel with 1000 rooms.

7.1.2   Boolean Arrays

The current state of the hotel rooms is defined by a list of boolean variables. In computing, such a list is called a *boolean array*. The array consists of a fixed number of boolean variables, which are known as the *array elements*.

The introduction of arrays in a programming language raises notational issues:

- How do you define an array in a program?

- How can a program perform the same action on every array element?

A mathematician might propose the following notation for a boolean array:

```
boolean free₁, free₂, ..., free₁₀;
```

and refer to a specific element as `free`$_i$. The element number i is called the *element index*.

A mathematician would also find it natural to use an *index variable* i to examine every element of the array, for example, by writing,

```
for (i = 1, 2, ..., 10)
    if (freeᵢ) out.writeln("Room " + i + " is free");
```

In mathematical texts, *ellipsis* points ... indicate the omission of (obvious) details, and indices are typeset as *subscripts*. Since a compiler cannot supply missing details in a program text, and subscripts are unavailable on

ASCII keyboards, the notation must be changed slightly before it can be included in a programming language.

In Java, the following statement defines a boolean array, named `free`:

```
boolean free[] = new boolean[10];
```

The array consists of 10 elements denoted

```
free[0] free[1] ... free[9]
```

Every element `free[i]` has an index i and a boolean value. The index is an integer in the range $0 \leq i \leq 9$. The value can be used in expressions and changed by assignments.

The `for` statement

```
for (i = 0; i <= 9; i++) free[i] = true;
```

assigns the value `true` to every element of the array.

After this initialization, the array can be visualized as a *table* of boolean values:

true	true	true	true	true	true	true	true	true	true
0	1	2	3	4	5	6	7	8	9

In Java programs, array indices always start at 0. Personally, I prefer to use indices from 1 to 10. So I will extend the array with an additional element (and ignore the first element):

---	true	true	true	true	true	true	true	true	true	true
0	1	2	3	4	5	6	7	8	9	10

The array can now be defined and initialized as follows:

```
int n = 10 /* rooms */;
boolean free[] = new boolean[n+1];
for (i = 1; i <= n; i++) free[i] = true;
```

Notice that the number of rooms can easily be changed to 1000 by redefining the integer constant n.

From now on, I will simplify array pictures by omitting the unused element:

true	true	true	true	true	true	true	true	true	true
1	2	3	4	5	6	7	8	9	10

The hotel program uses a random number generator to simulate the arrival of several guests. When the first guest has checked into, say, room number 8, the corresponding array element `free[8]` is assigned the value `false`:

true	true	true	true	true	true	true	false	true	true
1	2	3	4	5	6	7	8	9	10

When other guests have checked into rooms 1, 2, 3, 5, and 10, there are four free rooms left:

false	false	false	true	false	true	true	false	true	false
1	2	3	4	5	6	7	8	9	10

The initial `for` statement scans the array elements in their *natural order* (defined by the indices). In this case, the array elements are *accessed sequentially* (like the characters in a text file). However, the most important property of an array is that its elements can be accessed in *arbitrary order*. This enables the hotel program to select any room directly:

```
random choice = new random(1, n);
int room = choice.readint();
free[room] = false;
```

In general, the index of any array element `free[e]` is defined by an integer expression `e` with a value from 1 to 10. Since the expression

```
choice.readint()
```

yields an integer value in that range, the above statements can be replaced by a single assignment:

```
free[choice.readint()] = false;
```

The program makes *random reservations* by repeating this assignment 8 times:

```
int m = 8 /* guests */;
random choice = new random(1, n);
for (j = 1; j <= m; j++)
  free[choice.readint()] = false;
```

Since there is an element of chance in this program, it will normally reserve different rooms every time it is executed. In one instance, only 6 rooms were occupied after 8 arrivals. This happened because the random number generator (by chance) repeated some room numbers. In this program, it doesn't matter, since I am just trying to create any random mixture of free and occupied rooms.

At this point, the program scans all rooms

```
for (i = 1; i <= n; i++)
  if (free[i]) out.writeln("Room " + i + " is free");
```

and outputs a list of the *free rooms*

```
Room 4 is free
Room 6 is free
Room 7 is free
Room 9 is free
```

7.1.3 Searching a Table

Now comes the difficult part: when the next customer arrives, how does the program search the array for a free room?

An obvious idea is to examine all hotel rooms and record the index of a free room (if any) in a variable i:

```
int i;
for (j = 1; j <= n; j++)
  if (free[j]) i = j;
out.writeln("Room " + i + " is free");
```

This works if there is at least one free room. But, if all rooms are occupied, the loop never assigns a value to the variable i. In this situation, the program outputs the (unpredictable) number of an occupied (or non-existing) room.

We can remove this error by using any valid room number, say, 1, as the initial value of i, and checking if the final value of i refers to a free room:

```
int i = 1;
for (j = 1; j <= n; j++)
  if (free[j]) i = j;
if (free[i]) out.writeln("Room " + i + " is free");
else out.writeln("There is no free room");
```

After the random reservations (illustrated previously), there were four free rooms. The above statements will choose the *last free room* and display the message:

```
Room 9 is free
```

The most serious objection to this searching method is that it is unnecessary to examine every room to find one that is free (unless all of them are occupied). This may not matter for a small array. But a *telephone directory* would be useless if you had to read every name listed to find a phone number. And so would a *dictionary*.

A discussion of efficient search methods (Sedgewick 1983) is beyond the scope of this book. But I can at least show you another search method that is somewhat more efficient. This method is also a *linear search*, which scans the rooms in their natural order. But the search ends as soon as it finds the *first free room*. In the previous example, it would find that

```
Room 4 is free
```

The following (naive) loop includes a "lurking bug":

```
i = 1;
while (!free[i]) i = i + 1;
```

Most of the time (when the hotel is not full), the search works. But, if all 10 rooms are occupied, the search examines every room. When i reaches 10, the condition !free[i] is still true. So the body of the loop increases i one more time. The index now refers to a non-existing array element free[11]. Since this is meaningless, the program (fortunately) *halts* with the message

```
array index out of bounds: 11
```

This example illustrates one of the major pitfalls of array processing: *programs must ensure that array indices remain within the bounds of the corresponding index ranges.*

Suppose you add another condition to ensure that the control variable does not go beyond the end of the array:

```
i = 1;
while (!free[i] & (i <= n)) i = i + 1;
```

Unfortunately, this version crashes for the same reason. When the index reaches n, the condition i <= n is still true. So the body again increments the index i to n + 1 and causes abrupt termination when the program attempts to access the (non-existing) element `free[n+1]`.

The third version only increments the array index when it is less than n. Consequently, the index can never exceed n:

```
i = 1;
while (!free[i] & (i < n)) i = i + 1;
if (free[i]) out.writeln("Room " + i + " is free");
else out.writeln("There is no free room");
```

If the first n − 1 rooms are occupied, the loop terminates with i == n. However, we don't know if `free[n]` was found to be `true` or `false`. So we must again examine the chosen room `free[i]` to determine if it is free or not. This one works!

7.1.4 The Program "Hotel Rooms"

The complete hotel program illustrates the definition and use of a boolean array. The program uses my own variant of linear search which I encourage you to study until you understand it (Brinch Hansen 1990).

Program 7.1 *Hotel Rooms.*

```
/* Starts with n free hotel rooms, and makes m random
   reservations before finding another free room.
*/

class rooms extends basic
{ public static void main(String param[]) throws Exception
  { output out = new output("results");
    int m = 8 /* guests */, n = 10 /* rooms */;
    random choice = new random(1, n);
    boolean free[] = new boolean[n+1];
    int i, j;
    /* Start With All Rooms Free */
    for (i = 1; i <= n; i++) free[i] = true;
    /* Make Random Reservations */
    for (j = 1; j <= m; j++)
      free[choice.readint()] = false;
    /* List All Free Rooms */
    for (i = 1; i <= n; i++)
      if (free[i]) out.writeln("Room " + i + " is free");
    out.writeln();
    /* Find A Free Room (If Any) */
    i = 1; j = n;
    while (i < j)
      if (free[i]) j = i;
```

```
        else i = i + 1;
      if (free[i]) out.writeln("Room " + i + " is free");
      else out.writeln("There is no free room");
      out.close();
   }
}
```

7.2 TEXT ANALYSIS

Dictionaries use an interesting mixture of random and sequential access to make it easier to search for a word, such as `eisteddfod`. A *thumb index* immediately locates words beginning with `e` or `f`. *Alphabetic ordering* of these words narrows the search further, until you find a page with all words from `egregious` to `ejecta`. On this page, you will discover that `eisteddfod` is an annual competition among singers and poets in Wales (which was news to me).

Unfortunately, the words of English (or any other language) are not evenly divided among the letters of the alphabet. My English dictionary has 58 pages of words beginning with `e` but only 18 pages of words beginning with `k`. The uneven *distribution of letters* reduces the efficiency of a thumb index.

To collect data about the distribution of letters, I will write a program that inputs a text file and computes the relative frequency of occurrence of each letter. A capital letter is counted as the corresponding small letter.

When this program scans a text, it outputs a table of the form shown below. Due to rounding errors, the sum of the relative letter frequencies is not exactly 100 percent.

```
Letter Number Percent
--------------------
   a    2184      8
   b     513      2
   c     865      3
   d     881      3
   e    3505     12
   f     573      2
   g     630      2
   h     966      3
   i    2246      8
   j      43      0
   k     193      1
   l    1111      4
   m     930      3
   n    2317      8
   o    1989      7
   p     912      3
   q      32      0
   r    1786      6
   s    1694      6
   t    3180     11
   u     919      3
   v     288      1
   w     386      1
   x     187      1
   y     390      1
   z      25      0
--------------------
Total 28745     99
```

7.2.1 Integer Arrays

The program inputs a text file and counts the `total` number of letters in an integer variable (initialized to zero):

```
int total = 0;
```

An array is used to count the **number** of times each letter occurs:

```
int number[] = new int[...];
```

This array consists of a fixed number of integer elements. The question is how many elements do we need and how should they be indexed?

If we use the *ordinal values* of the 128 ASCII characters as indices in this table, the letters will be counted in elements **97** to **122** (see Table 6.1). This insight leads me to define an array of 123 elements:

```
int number[] = new int[123];
```

of which only the last 26 will be used:

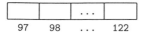

In this table, the letter a is counted in element

`number[97]`

which is the same as the element

`number[(ord)'a']`

When a character occurs in an index expression, it is automatically converted to its ordinal value (see 6.6.2). So the above element can simply be denoted

`number['a']`

It should now be obvious that we may as well regard the useful part of the array as 26 *integer elements* with *character indices* from 'a' to 'z'. The following picture shows this part of the array when the elements have been initialized to zero:

In Java, this array is defined and initialized as follows:

```
int number[] = new int['z'+1];
for (char ch = 'a'; ch <= 'z'; ch++)
  number[ch] = 0;
```

The program inputs one character at a time and counts the letters only:

```
while (in.more())
  { char ch = in.read();
    if (('a' <= ch) & (ch <= 'z'))
      { number[ch] = number[ch] + 1;
        total = total + 1;
      }
    else if (('A' <= ch) & (ch <= 'Z'))
      { ch = (char)(ch - 'A' + 'a');
        number[ch] = number[ch] + 1;
        total = total + 1;
      }
  }
```

The conversion of a capital letter to the corresponding small letter is similar to the opposite conversion (see 6.6.2).

7.2.2 Real Numbers

When the program analyzed a text of about 1400 lines, it counted a `total` of 28745 letters. The following array picture shows the total number of the letters a, b, and z:

2184	513	...	25
'a'	'b'	...	'z'

The relative frequency of the letter a is 2184/28745, which is 0.076. However, since *integer division* ignores the fractional part without rounding the result, we obtain a (meaningless) zero instead (see 1.5.1).

To prevent the complete loss of significant digits, we must convert the two integers to the corresponding *real numbers* and compute a real fraction 2184.0/28745.0, which indeed is 0.076. The percentage of 'a's is obtained by multiplying this quotient by 100.0, which gives 7.6 percent.

When this fraction is converted to an integer, the (truncated) result is 7 percent. Instead, I will *round* the result by adding 0.5 to the percentage before the type conversion. This gives 8.1 percent. The corresponding integer result is 8 percent, which is close enough.

In Java, a real number is represented by a data type known as a `double`. The *type conversion*

```
(double)total
```

converts the integer value `total` to the corresponding `double` value. The `fraction` of all letters that are 'e's is

```
double fraction = (double)number['e']/(double)total;
```

The corresponding percentage is 100.0*`fraction`. This result is rounded and converted to the nearest integer:

```
int pct = (int)(100.0*fraction + 0.5);
```

Since real numbers only play an occasional role in this book, I will not discuss them further at this point.

7.2.3   The Program "Letter Distribution"

This completes the development of the program that analyzes the letter
distribution in a text file.

Program 7.2 *Letter Distribution.*

```
/* Reads a text file and computes the relative
   frequency of occurrence of each letter. Only
   letters are counted. A capital letter is
   counted as the corresponding small letter.
*/

class letters extends basic
{ public static void main(String param[]) throws Exception
  { input in = new input("chapter1");
    output out = new output("results");
    int number[] = new int['z'+1];
    for (char ch = 'a'; ch <= 'z'; ch++)
      number[ch] = 0;
    int total = 0;
    while (in.more())
      { char ch = in.read();
        if (('a' <= ch) & (ch <= 'z'))
          { number[ch] = number[ch] + 1;
            total = total + 1;
          }
        else if (('A' <= ch) & (ch <= 'Z'))
          { ch = (char)(ch - 'A' + 'a');
            number[ch] = number[ch] + 1;
            total = total + 1;
          }
      }
    out.writeln("Letter Number Percent");
    out.writeln("--------------------");
    int sum = 0;
    for (char ch = 'a'; ch <= 'z'; ch++)
      { double fraction = (double)number[ch]/(double)total;
        int pct = (int)(100.0*fraction + 0.5);
        out.write("    " + ch);
        out.write(number[ch], 8);
        out.writeln(pct, 6);
        sum = sum + pct;
      }
    out.writeln("--------------------");
    out.write("Total", 6);
    out.write(total, 6);
    out.writeln(sum, 6);
    in.close(); out.close();
  }
}
```

7.2.4 Non-Nested Blocks

Program 7.2 defines three variables with the same name ch:

```
 1 { ...
 2   for (char ch = 'a'; ch <= 'z'; ch++)
 3     number[ch] = 0;
 4   ...
 5   while (in.more())
 6     { char ch = in.read();
 7       if (('a' <= ch) & (ch <= 'z'))
 8         { number[ch] = number[ch] + 1;
 9           ...
10         }
11       else if (('A' <= ch) & (ch <= 'Z'))
12         { ch = (char)(ch - 'A' + 'a');
13           number[ch] = number[ch] + 1;
14           ...
15         }
16     }
17   ...
18   for (char ch = 'a'; ch <= 'z'; ch++)
19     { double fraction = (double)number[ch]/(double)total;
20       ...
21       out.write("   " + ch);
22       out.write(number[ch], 7);
23       ...
24     }
25   ...
27 }
```

The following table shows the scope of these variables. To be able to distinguish between them, they are called ch$'$, ch$''$, and ch$'''$ in the table.

Variable	Known in lines
ch$'$	2–3
ch$''$	6–16
ch$'''$	18–24

The body of the **while** statement is a block. The two **for** statements are also regarded as blocks (see 5.4). So we have three non-nested blocks, each of which defines a local variable, named ch. For such a program, the following rule applies:

- *If non-nested blocks define variables of the same name, they are considered different variables.*

From the standard *scope rules*, it follows that *each variable is known only inside the block that defines it* (see 5.3.1).

7.3   JAVA PITFALLS

My explanation of *array variables* is only correct if you impose the following restrictions on your use of this concept. Any program that violates these restrictions can have unexpected results, which are not detected during compilation or execution.

- **Do not use the assignment operator for array variables.**

Example:

```
boolean free[] = new boolean[n+1];
boolean vacant[] = new boolean[n+1];
vacant = free;
```

Instead, copy an array, element by element:

```
for (int i = 1; i <= n; i++) vacant[i] = free[i];
```

- **Do not use comparison operators for array variables.**

Example:

```
boolean free[] = new boolean[n+1];
boolean vacant[] = new boolean[n+1];
if (vacant == free) ...
```

Instead, compare two arrays, element by element, using a variant of linear search (see 7.1.4):

```
int i = 1, j = n;
while (i < j)
  if (free[i] != vacant[i]) j = i;
  else i = i + 1;
if (free[i] == vacant[i]) ...
```

7.4   PROGRAMMING EXERCISES

Exercise 7.1   Amnesty

A king grants partial amnesty to 10 prisoners, locked in individual prison cells. First, the jailer unlocks each of the 10 cells. Then starting with the second cell, he turns the key in every second cell. Then starting with the third cell, he turns the key in every third cell, and so forth. If a cell is unlocked, a turn of the key locks it (and vice versa). When the jailor is finished, the prisoners can leave if their doors are unlocked.

Write a Java program that finds and displays the cell numbers of the lucky prisoners.

Exercise 7.2 Find Anagrams

Write a Java program that reads a text file and writes another text file. Each input line consists of two different lower-case words separated by a space and followed by a newline character. For each line, the program copies the two words from the input file to the output file and writes a message indicating whether or not the second word is an anagram of the first word. An anagram is a word obtained by rearranging the letters in another word.

Use the following input text to test the program:

```
item time
acres caress
scare cares
react crater
```

Exercise 7.3 Find Pangrams

Write a Java program that reads a text file and writes another text file. Each input line consists of small letters and spaces only followed by a newline character. For each line, the program copies the line from the input file to the output file and writes a message indicating whether or not the line is a pangram. A pangram is a sentence that includes every letter of the alphabet.

Use the following input text to test the program:

```
the quick brown fox jumps over the lazy dog
the slow brown fox jumps over the lazy dog
```

Exercise 7.4 The Birthday Problem

Write a Java program that solves the birthday problem: If 23 people are in the same room, what is the chance that at least two of them were born on the same day of the year?

Simulate 10,000 different groups of 23 people each and output the number of groups in which some birthdays coincide.

Hint: assume that there are 365 days in a year. For each group of people, make a list of the 365 days of the year. Then, for each person, select a random birthday between 1 and 365, and put a checkmark next to that day. If any day of the year is marked more than once, then at least two of the people in that group have the same birthday.

Exercise 7.5 Nobel Prizes

Write a Java program that performs the following sequence of actions:

1. Input and store the following list of the 1950s Nobel Prizes in Literature:

```
1950  Britain, Bertrand Russell
1951  Sweden, Per Lagerkvist
1952  France, Francois Mauriac
1953  Britain, Winston Churchill
1954  USA, Ernest Hemingway
1955  Iceland, Halldor Laxness
1956  Spain, Juan Ramon Jimenez
1957  France, Albert Camus
1958  USSR, Boris Pasternak
1959  Italy, Salvatore Quasimodo
```

2. Ask the user to type the name of a country.

3. Scan the list and display the years and names of the winners (if any) from that country.

4. If any winners were found, go back to step 2; otherwise, terminate with a final message.

Exercise 7.6 Gift Ideas

Write a program that inputs the following text file:

```
15 Gift ideas:

Basketball        $15
Binoculars        $40
Boom_box          $90
Calculator        $20
Camera            $60
CD_player        $170
Clock_radio       $35
Color_TV         $330
Cordless_phone   $180
Gas_grill        $200
Hair_dryer        $23
Sewing_machine   $250
Skateboard        $30
Telescope        $100
Wall_clock       $130
```

The program makes random selections from this list of gift ideas. The selection of gifts ends as soon as their total price exceeds $500. *No gift may be selected more than once.* The output shows the gifts selected and their total price. *Hint:* use several arrays with elements of different types.

8

MATRICES

This chapter explores the use of *matrices* to compute two-dimensional tables.

8.1   RECTANGULAR MATRICES

8.1.1   A Spreadsheet Problem

I will write a program that inputs, adds, and prints the estimated cost of buying a small car and driving it 100,000 miles over 10 years (Federal Highway Administration 1980).

The input is a text file of 10 lines:

```
1979 14500  998 1780
1980 13000  985 1383
1981 11500 1031 1293
1982 10000 1008 1225
1983  9900 1060 1137
1984  9900 1297 1127
1985  9500 1428 1060
1986  8500  826  938
1987  7500  801 1056
1988  5700  458  826
```

For every year, the data show the miles driven, the cost of operating, and the cost of owning the car in that year.

The program inputs the data and computes column and row totals. The spreadsheet is then output with column headings:

YEAR	MILES DRIVEN	OPERATING COSTS	OWNING COSTS	TOTAL COSTS
1979	14500	998	1780	2778
1980	13000	985	1383	2368
1981	11500	1031	1293	2324
1982	10000	1008	1225	2233
1983	9900	1060	1137	2197
1984	9900	1297	1127	2424
1985	9500	1428	1060	2488
1986	8500	826	938	1764
1987	7500	801	1056	1857
1988	5700	458	826	1284
-------	------	----	-----	-----
1979-88	100000	9892	11825	21717

8.1.2   Integer Matrices

The program keeps the data in a table of the following form:

	1	2	3	4	5
1	1979	14500	998	1780	2778
2	1980	13000	985	1383	2368
3	1981	11500	1031	1293	2324
4	1982	10000	1008	1225	2233
5	1983	9900	1060	1137	2197
6	1984	9900	1297	1127	2424
7	1985	9500	1428	1060	2488
8	1986	8500	826	938	1764
9	1987	7500	801	1056	1857
10	1988	5700	458	826	1284
11		100000	9892	11825	21717

The computer stores the table in a *two-dimensional array*, known as an *integer matrix*. The matrix consists of 55 integer elements, arranged in 11 *rows* and 5 *columns*. Every *element* is an integer variable with a *value* and two *indices*—a *row number* (from 1 to 11) and a *column number* (from 1 to 5).

In Java, the following defines the integer matrix, named `table`:

```
int m = 11, n = 5;
int table[][] = new int[m+1][n+1];
```

Two constants m and n define the number of rows and columns *used* by the program.

Strictly speaking, the matrix has 12 rows (numbered 0 to 11) and 6 columns (numbered 0 to 5). I will, however, ignore row 0 and column 0, and think of it as an array with 11 rows and 5 columns numbered from 1.

The `table` is called an m × n matrix. Since m ≠ n, it is a *rectangular matrix*.

Every matrix element `table[i][j]` is identified by its row number i and column number j. As an example, in the present example `table[4][3]` has the value 1008.

8.1.3 Matrix Computation

The following `for` statements input the matrix elements, line by line, one integer at a time:

```
for (int i = 1; i <= m - 1; i++)
  for (int j = 1; j <= n - 1; j++)
    table[i][j] = in.readint();
```

The matrix now holds the values shown below:

	1	2	3	4	5
1	1979	14500	998	1780	
2	1980	13000	985	1383	
3	1981	11500	1031	1293	
4	1982	10000	1008	1225	
5	1983	9900	1060	1137	
6	1984	9900	1297	1127	
7	1985	9500	1428	1060	
8	1986	8500	826	938	
9	1987	7500	801	1056	
10	1988	5700	458	826	
11					

Row 11 and column 5 are *not* input. Indeed, the purpose of the spreadsheet program is to compute row and column totals and store them in these elements. This is done in two steps:

1. For each of the rows 1 to 10, elements 3 to 4 are added:

```
for (int i = 1; i <= m - 1; i++)
  { int sum = 0;
    for (int j = 3; j <= n - 1; j++)
      sum = sum + table[i][j];
    table[i][n] = sum;
  }
```

The row totals are assigned to the corresponding elements in column **5**:

	1	2	3	4	5
1	1979	14500	998	1780	2778
2	1980	13000	985	1383	2368
3	1981	11500	1031	1293	2324
4	1982	10000	1008	1225	2233
5	1983	9900	1060	1137	2197
6	1984	9900	1297	1127	2424
7	1985	9500	1428	1060	2488
8	1986	8500	826	938	1764
9	1987	7500	801	1056	1857
10	1988	5700	458	826	1284
11					

2. For each of the columns 2 to 5, elements 1 to 10 are added:

```
for (int j = 2; j <= n; j++)
  { int sum = 0;
    for (int i = 1; i <= m - 1; i++)
      sum = sum + table[i][j];
    table[m][j] = sum;
  }
```

The column sums are assigned to the corresponding elements in row **11**:

	1	2	3	4	5
1	1979	14500	998	1780	2778
2	1980	13000	985	1383	2368
3	1981	11500	1031	1293	2324
4	1982	10000	1008	1225	2233
5	1983	9900	1060	1137	2197
6	1984	9900	1297	1127	2424
7	1985	9500	1428	1060	2488
8	1986	8500	826	938	1764
9	1987	7500	801	1056	1857
10	1988	5700	458	826	1284
11		100000	9892	11825	21717

8.1.4   The Program "Spreadsheet"

The remaining details concern the *output* of the spreadsheet (see 1.6.3).

Program 8.1 *Spreadsheet.*

```
/* Inputs, sums, and prints a spreadsheet showing the
   cost of buying a small car and driving it 100,000
   miles over 10 years.
     The input is a text file of 10 lines, one for
   each year. Each line defines the corresponding
   year, the miles driven, the operating costs, and
   the ownership costs for that year.
     The program inputs the data in an integer matrix
   and computes relevant column and row totals. The
   spreadsheet is then output with column headings.
*/

class spreadsheet extends basic
{ public static void main(String param[]) throws Exception
  { input in = new input("data/spreadsheet");
    output out = new output("results");
    int m = 11, n = 5;
    int table[][] = new int[m+1][n+1];
    /* Input Data */
    for (int i = 1; i <= m - 1; i++)
      for (int j = 1; j <= n - 1; j++)
        table[i][j] = in.readint();
    /* Add Rows */
    for (int i = 1; i <= m - 1; i++)
      { int sum = 0;
        for (int j = 3; j <= n - 1; j++)
          sum = sum + table[i][j];
        table[i][n] = sum;
      }
    /* Add Columns */
    for (int j = 2; j <= n; j++)
      { int sum = 0;
        for (int i = 1; i <= m - 1; i++)
          sum = sum + table[i][j];
        table[m][j] = sum;
      }
    /* Output spreadsheet */
    out.writeln("      YEAR      MILES" +
       "   OPERATING  OWNING     TOTAL");
    out.writeln("                     DRIVEN" +
       "     COSTS     COSTS     COSTS");
    out.writeln();
    int width = 10;
    for (int i = 1; i <= m - 1; i++)
      { for (int j = 1; j <= n; j++)
          out.write(table[i][j], width);
        out.writeln();
      }
    out.writeln("     -------    ------" +
```

```
     "        ----       -----        -----");
  out.write("   1979-88");
  for (int j = 2; j <= n; j++)
    out.write(table[m][j], width);
  out.writeln();
  in.close(); out.close();
   }
 }
```

8.2 SQUARE MATRICES

8.2.1 A Crossword Puzzle

Hangman is a game in which one player chooses a word and the others try
to guess it one letter at a time. I have come up with a variant of this game.

You have, say, 24 guesses to determine the letters in the secret solution
to a *crossword puzzle*. The program inputs the correct solution from a text
file and stores it in a character matrix. Every time you choose a letter, the
puzzle is displayed showing the letters you have guessed so far. The program
ends if you either solve the puzzle, or run out of guesses.

As an example, here is an *input file* with the solution to a 13×13 crossword puzzle (Good Time Crossword Puzzles 1997):

```
13

b a a . h o o . . t r a p
e l f . i r a n . i o t a
t e a . p e t e . a w e d
s c r a p . h e a r . . .
. . . d o g . . s a g a s
a l p s . r u s h . i c e
r i o . m o r a y . v e t
t e e . o w n s . b e d s
s u m a . . . s k i . . .
. . . s k i d . e n s u e
a i r s . t i d y . e n d
f r e e . e r i e . a d e
t e n t . m e n d . l o n
```

After inputting this file (without displaying it), the program asked me to
Type the maximum number of guesses. I typed 24 and was immediately
asked to Type a letter. To improve my chances of winning the game, I
decided to select letters according to their frequency of occurrence (see 7.2).

My (obvious) first choice was the letter e. The program responded by
displaying a partial solution to the puzzle showing where the 'e's occur:

```
? ? ? . ? ? ? . . ? ? ? ?
e ? ? . ? ? ? ? . ? ? ? ?
? e ? . ? e ? e . ? ? e ?
? ? ? ? ? . ? e ? ? . . .
. . . ? ? ? . . ? ? ? ? ?
? ? ? ? . ? ? ? ? . ? ? e
? ? ? . ? ? ? ? ? . ? e ?
? e e . ? ? ? ? . ? e ? ?
? ? ? ? . . . ? ? ? . . .
. . . ? ? ? ? . e ? ? ? e
? ? ? ? . ? ? ? ? . e ? ?
? ? e e . e ? ? e   ? ? e
? e ? ? . ? e ? ? . ? ? ?
```

The remaining unknown letters are shown as question marks.

My second choice was a t, which extended the partial solution a bit:

```
? ? ? . ? ? ? . . t ? ? ?
e ? ? . ? ? ? ? . ? ? t ?
t e ? . ? e t e . ? ? e ?
? ? ? ? ? . ? e ? ? . . .
. . . ? ? ? . . ? ? ? ? ?
? ? ? ? . ? ? ? ? . ? ? e
? ? ? . ? ? ? ? ? . ? e t
t e e . ? ? ? ? . ? e ? ?
? ? ? ? . . . ? ? ? . . .
. . . ? ? ? ? . e ? ? ? e
? ? ? ? . t ? ? ? . e ? ?
? ? e e . e ? ? e . ? ? e
t e ? t . ? e ? ? . ? ? ?
```

and so forth.

My 22nd choice was an x, which, as you can see below, does not occur anywhere. In this case, the program just displayed the 21st partial solution again:

```
b a a . h o o . . t r a p
e l f . i r a n . i o t a
t e a . p e t e . a w e d
s c r a p . h e a r . . .
. . . d o g . . s a g a s
a l p s . r u s h . i c e
r i o . m o r a ? . v e t
t e e . o w n s . b e d s
s u m a . . . s k i . . .
. . . s k i d . e n s u e
a i r s . t i d ? . e n d
f r e e . e r i e . a d e
t e n t . m e n d . l o n
```

When I typed the letter y, the program displayed the complete solution:

```
b a a . h o o . . t r a p
e l f . i r a n . i o t a
t e a . p e t e . a w e d
s c r a p . h e a r . . .
. . . d o g . . s a g a s
a l p s . r u s h . i c e
r i o . m o r a y . v e t
t e e . o w n s . b e d s
s u m a . . . s k i . . .
. . . s k i d . e n s u e
a i r s . t i d y . e n d
f r e e . e r i e . a d e
t e n t . m e n d . l o n
```

and wrote: You won after 23 guesses. This is pretty good, considering that this crossword puzzle uses all letters in the English alphabet (except j, q, x, and z). Consequently, it is impossible to solve it in less than 22 guesses.

8.2.2   Character Matrices

The program keeps the complete and partial solutions to the crossword puzzle in two character matrices.

In this example, the matrix that holds the *hidden solution* to the puzzle is a *square matrix* consisting of 13×13 character variables.

	1	2	3	4	5	6	7	8	9	10	11	12	13
1	'b'	'a'	'a'	'.'	'h'	'o'	'o'	'.'	'.'	't'	'r'	'a'	'p'
2	'e'	'l'	'f'	'.'	'i'	'r'	'a'	'n'	'.'	'i'	'o'	't'	'a'
3	't'	'e'	'a'	'.'	'p'	'e'	't'	'e'	'.'	'a'	'w'	'e'	'd'
4	's'	'c'	'r'	'a'	'p'	'.'	'h'	'e'	'a'	'r'	'.'	'.'	'.'
5	'.'	'.'	'.'	'd'	'o'	'g'	'.'	'.'	's'	'a'	'g'	'a'	's'
6	'a'	'l'	'p'	's'	'.'	'r'	'u'	's'	'h'	'.'	'i'	'c'	'e'
7	'r'	'i'	'o'	'.'	'm'	'o'	'r'	'a'	'y'	'.'	'v'	'e'	't'
8	't'	'e'	'e'	'.'	'o'	'w'	'n'	's'	'.'	'b'	'e'	'd'	's'
9	's'	'u'	'm'	'a'	'.'	'.'	'.'	's'	'k'	'i'	'.'	'.'	'.'
10	'.'	'.'	'.'	's'	'k'	'i'	'd'	'.'	'e'	'n'	's'	'u'	'e'
11	'a'	'i'	'r'	's'	'.'	't'	'i'	'd'	'y'	'.'	'e'	'n'	'd'
12	'f'	'r'	'e'	'e'	'.'	'e'	'r'	'i'	'e'	'.'	'a'	'd'	'e'
13	't'	'e'	'n'	't'	'.'	'm'	'e'	'n'	'd'	'.'	'l'	'o'	'n'
	1	2	3	4	5	6	7	8	9	10	11	12	13

The matrix that holds the *partial solution* is initialized with question marks and periods only:

	1	2	3	4	5	6	7	8	9	10	11	12	13
1	'?'	'?'	'?'	'.'	'?'	'?'	'?'	'.'	'.'	'?'	'?'	'?'	'?'
2	'?'	'?'	'?'	'.'	'?'	'?'	'?'	'?'	'.'	'?'	'?'	'?'	'?'
3	'?'	'?'	'?'	'.'	'?'	'?'	'?'	'?'	'.'	'?'	'?'	'?'	'?'
4	'?'	'?'	'?'	'?'	'?'	'.'	'?'	'?'	'?'	'?'	'.'	'.'	'.'
5	'.'	'.'	'.'	'?'	'?'	'?'	'.'	'.'	'?'	'?'	'?'	'?'	'?'
6	'?'	'?'	'?'	'?'	'.'	'?'	'?'	'?'	'?'	'.'	'?'	'?'	'?'
7	'?'	'?'	'?'	'.'	'?'	'?'	'?'	'?'	'?'	'.'	'?'	'?'	'?'
8	'?'	'?'	'?'	'.'	'?'	'?'	'?'	'?'	'.'	'?'	'?'	'?'	'?'
9	'?'	'?'	'?'	'?'	'.'	'.'	'.'	'?'	'?'	'?'	'.'	'.'	'.'
10	'.'	'.'	'.'	'?'	'?'	'?'	'?'	'.'	'?'	'?'	'?'	'?'	'?'
11	'?'	'?'	'?'	'?'	'.'	'?'	'?'	'?'	'?'	'.'	'?'	'?'	'?'
12	'?'	'?'	'?'	'?'	'.'	'?'	'?'	'?'	'?'	'.'	'?'	'?'	'?'
13	'?'	'?'	'?'	'?'	'.'	'?'	'?'	'?'	'?'	'.'	'?'	'?'	'?'

These two character matrices, named a and b, are defined as follows:

```
int n = data.readint();
assume (n >= 1);
char a[][] = new char[n+1][n+1];
char b[][] = new char[n+1][n+1];
```

Each array can hold a crossword puzzle of up to n × n characters. The program inputs the dimension of the puzzle in an integer variable n.

8.2.3 Conditional Expressions

The initialization of the arrays uses an elegant idea, called a *conditional expression*:

```
for (int i = 1; i <= n; i++)
  for (int j = 1; j <= n; j++)
    { data.readblanks();
      char ch = data.read();
      a[i][j] = ch;
      b[i][j] = (ch == '.' ? '.' : '?');

    }
```

The conditional expression

```
(ch == '.' ? '.' : '?')
```

defines a character value: if the character ch is a period, the value of the conditional expression is also a period; otherwise, the value is a question mark.

In general, a conditional expression

```
(B ? e : f)
```

consists of a *boolean expression* B and two expressions e and f of the same type. If B is true, the value of the conditional expression is e; otherwise, it is f.

8.2.4   Another Matrix Computation

The program is now ready to let the user choose letters as long as the game is in progress:

```
GuessPuzzle:
  StartTheGame
  while (InProgress)
    { ChooseALetter
      UpdatePartial
      CompleteGuess
    }
```

The user starts the game by selecting the maximum number of guesses:

```
StartTheGame:
  out.writeln("Type the maximum number of guesses");
  int max = in.readint(), guesses = 0, known = 0;
```

Initially, the number of character fields known by the user is zero.

The game continues as long as the number of known characters is less than the total number of characters, *and* the maximum number of guesses has not been reached:

```
InProgress:
  (known < n*n) & (guesses < max)
```

The user chooses a letter as follows:

```
ChooseALetter:
  out.writeln("Type a letter");
  out.writeln();
  in.readblanks();
  char ch = in.read();
```

When the user has chosen the next letter `ch`, the program scans the matrix `a`, which holds the complete solution. Wherever the program finds the letter `ch` in `a`, it assigns the same letter to the corresponding element of the partial solution `b`. If the latter element is no longer a question mark, it is counted as a known character. (Note that this rule ensures that periods are counted as known characters.) The program outputs the partial solution, as it computes it.

```
UpdatePartial:
  known = 0;
  for (int i = 1; i <= n; i++)
    { for (int j = 1; j <= n; j++)
        { if (a[i][j] == ch) b[i][j] = ch;
          if (b[i][j] != '?') known = known + 1;
          out.write(b[i][j] + " ");
        }
      out.writeln();
    }
  out.writeln();
```

At the end of each guess, the total number of guesses is increased by one:

```
CompleteGuess:
  guesses = guesses + 1;
```

8.2.5 The Program "Hangman"

The complete program is obtained by putting the program pieces together and adding some trivial details:

Program 8.2 *Hangman.*

```
/* You have, say, 24 guesses to determine the letters
   in the secret solution to a crossword puzzle. The
   program inputs the correct solution from a text
   file and stores it in a character matrix. Every
   time you type a letter (followed by return), the
   puzzle is displayed showing the letters you guessed
   so far. The remaining unknown letters are shown as
   question marks. The program ends if you either solve
   the puzzle, or run out of guesses.
*/

class hangman extends basic
{ public static void main(String param[]) throws Exception
  { input data = new input("hangman");
    input in = new input();
    output out = new output();
```

```
      int n = data.readint();
      assume (n >= 1);
      char a[][] = new char[n+1][n+1];
      char b[][] = new char[n+1][n+1];
      for (int i = 1; i <= n; i++)
        for (int j = 1; j <= n; j++)
          { data.readblanks();
            char ch = data.read();
            a[i][j] = ch;
            b[i][j] = (ch == '.' ? '.' : '?');
          }
      out.writeln("Type the maximum number of guesses");
      int max = in.readint(), guesses = 0, known = 0;
      while ((known < n*n) & (guesses < max))
        { out.writeln("Type a letter");
          out.writeln();
          in.readblanks();
          char ch = in.read();
          known = 0;
          for (int i = 1; i <= n; i++)
            { for (int j = 1; j <= n; j++)
                { if (a[i][j] == ch) b[i][j] = ch;
                  if (b[i][j] != '?') known = known + 1;
                  out.write(b[i][j] + " ");
                }
              out.writeln();
            }
          out.writeln();
          guesses = guesses + 1;
        }
      out.writeln("You " + (known == n*n ? "won" : "lost")
        + " after " + guesses + " guesses");
      data.close(); in.close(); out.close();
    }
}
```

8.3 PROGRAMMING EXERCISES

Exercise 8.1 Magic Squares

A square array of integers is a magic square if the sums of the numbers in each row, column, and diagonal are the same. Write a Java program that uses an $n \times n$ matrix of integers. First, the program inputs the matrix values from a text file. (The user types the file name on the keyboard.) The program then displays the matrix values on the screen (with nicely aligned columns). Finally, the program checks if the matrix is magic and displays the message, magic square (or non-magic square) on the screen.

Use the following matrices to test the program for $n = 4$:

```
 1 12  7 14          1 12  7 14
 8 13  2 11          8 13  2 11
10  3 16  5         10  3 16  5
15  6  9  4         15  6  9  3
```

Exercise 8.2 The Game of Life

On a chessboard, each square represents a cell which is either alive or dead. If you count the sides which a cell shares with other cells, then each cell is in touch with four neighbors (unless it is at the edge of the board).

Write a Java program that uses a matrix with n × n elements to represent the cells, where n = 45. First the program marks the cells on the two diagonals as alive and the rest of the cells as dead. The program then scans the board n times. During each scan, it updates all the cells as follows: If a cell has one, two or three living neighbors the cell is marked as alive; otherwise it is dead. (Notice that this rule permits dead cells to become alive.)

After the nth step, the program outputs a two-dimensional image of the final, updated board. Each cell is printed as an asterisk if it is alive and as a space if it is dead.

Exercise 8.3 Submarine Hunt

Write a Java program that simulates a submarine hunt. Your aim is to force a submerged submarine to surface by hitting it with a depth charge. Your radar image of the ocean is a 5 × 5 matrix of characters. The submarine is hidden somewhere in this matrix. The fixed position of the submarine is chosen at random by the program.

Initially, the program displays a blank radar screen with row and column numbers (Figure 1). The submarine is hidden below the surface and does not appear on the radar screen.

You can now drop one depth charge at a time. When you type two numbers, say 3 4 (followed by return), a depth charge is dropped in row 3 and column 4. If you do not hit the submarine, the radar image is displayed again with a - sign in that spot (Figure 2).

If you hit the submarine after dropping, say, three depth charges, the submarine floats to the surface and appears on the radar screen as an x (Figure 3).

```
  1 2 3 4 5          1 2 3 4 5          1 2 3 4 5
1 . . . . .        1 . . . . .        1 . . . . -
2 . . . . .        2 . . . . .        2 . x . . .
3 . . . . .        3 . . . - .        3 . . . - .
4 . . . . .        4 . . . . .        4 . . . . .
5 . . . . .        5 . . . . .        5 . . . . .

   Figure 1            Figure 2            Figure 3
```

You have 10 depth charges. The game ends when you either hit the submarine or run out of depth charges.

Exercise 8.4   Tic-Tac-Toe

Write a Java program that plays a simplified form of tic-tac-toe with the user. The program performs the following sequence of actions:

1. The program displays an empty board with three rows and three columns. The empty squares are marked by periods.

2. The user is asked to type either a row number and a column number, or the word `stop`.

3. If the user types `stop`, the program proceeds to step 7; otherwise, it continues with step 4.

4. The program selects an empty square at random.

5. The board is displayed again. The squares selected by the user and the program are marked `X` and `0`, respectively.

6. The program continues at step 2.

7. The program asks you to decide who won. This ends the game.

The figures below illustrate the input and output after each move by the user and the program:

```
INPUT              2 2      1 3      3 1      stop

OUTPUT    . . .    . . .    . . X    . 0 X    you decide who won
          . . .    0 X .    0 X 0    0 X 0
          . . .    . . .    . . .    X . .
```

Exercise 8.5   Jungle

A chessboard represents a jungle populated only by elephants and tigers. Each square can be occupied by either an elephant or a tiger. If you count the sides that a square shares with other squares, then each animal is surrounded by four neighboring animals (unless it is at the edge of the jungle).

Write a Java program that uses a 10×10 matrix to represent the jungle. Initially the program generates a random distribution of elephants and tigers. The program then scans the board 100 times. During each scan, the following rules decide the fate of each animal: (1) if an elephant is surrounded by three or four tigers, it dies and is immediately replaced at random by a new tiger or elephant; otherwise, the elephant stays alive. (2) A similar rule applies to tigers. (3) You decide how to handle an animal at the edge of the jungle.

After the last scan, the program outputs a two-dimensional image of the jungle showing the final distribution of animals. Each square is printed as an `E` if it is occupied by an elephant and as a `T` is it is occupied by a tiger.

9

METHODS

This chapter introduces the *method* concept, which assigns a name to a block statement. The method name serves as an *abbreviation* for the block statement and makes it possible to use the same statement in different places without copying it.

9.1 PROGRAM COMPOSITION

Divide and conquer is the essence of human problem solving. This thinking process involves two stages:

- *Decomposition*: First you divide a complex problem into simpler problems, which are then solved one at a time.

- *Composition*: Then you combine the solutions to the subproblems into a solution to the whole problem.

This is what a mathematician does when she proves minor mathematical propositions (*lemmas*) separately and uses them to prove a major proposition (a *theorem*). This is what I do when I divide this book into *chapters*, which can be written individually. It is also what you do when you use *stepwise programming* to break a computation into smaller parts, which can be programmed one at a time and combined into a complete program.

Since a programming language is a *thinking tool*, it should include notational concepts for combining smaller units into larger ones. So far you have used two kinds of *composition mechanisms*:

- *structured statements*: if, switch, for, while, and block statements;

- *data structures*: text files, strings, and arrays.

We now add another composition mechanism to our toolkit, the *method*, which enables you to assign a name to a block statement and use it as a new operation.

You are already familiar with the read and write methods defined by the Java text program. Now you will learn to define and use methods in your own Java programs.

9.2   SIMPLE FUNCTIONS

A *function* is a method that defines the computation of a value.

9.2.1   The Function Concept

Program 6.3 uses the following statement to replace a small letter ch by the corresponding capital letter:

```
if (('a' <= ch) & (ch <= 'z'))
   out.write((char)(ch - 'a' + 'A'));
```

To make this statement easier to read, I will define two functions, named small and capital, and rewrite it as follows:

```
if (small(ch)) out.write(capital(ch));
```

The function small determines whether or not a character ch is a small letter. The function capital converts a small letter ch to the corresponding capital letter.

The first function can be used to examine *any* character and compute a boolean value: if the character is a small letter, the function value is true; otherwise, it is false.

The use of this function to classify a character, say,

```
small('p')
```

is an *abbreviation* for a boolean expression, in this case

```
('a' <= 'p') & ('p' <= 'z')
```

Since 'p' is a character between 'a' and 'z', the value of this expression is true.

To paraphrase a familiar saying about ducks: if it looks like an expression and behaves like an expression, then it *is* an expression. It is only common sense that we should regard the abbreviation

```
small('p')
```

itself as a boolean expression. This kind of expression is known as a *function designator*. The execution of a function designator is called a *function invocation* or a *function call*. (To *invoke*, from the Latin word *invocare*, means "to call.") The character value 'p' is known as the *actual parameter* of the function call. The invocation is said to *return* a boolean function value.

Here are some examples of function designators and their values:

Function designator	Actual parameter	Function value
small('p')	'p'	true
small('D')	'D'	false
small('$')	'$'	false

The function small is defined as follows:

```
static boolean small(char x)
{ return ('a' <= x) & (x <= 'z'); }
```

Every call of this function computes the value of the boolean expression

```
('a' <= x) & (x <= 'z')
```

for a particular character x. Since the function can be applied to *any* character value, the function uses a *generic name* x to refer to the actual parameter value in a particular function call.

The operand x plays the same role as an *unknown quantity* in a mathematical equation. To evaluate such an equation, you must replace the unknown quantity by a known quantity.

If you replace the unknown quantity x in the boolean expression

```
('a' <= x) & (x <= 'z')
```

by a known character value, say, 'p', you obtain the expression

```
('a' <= 'p') & ('p' <= 'z')
```

in which all the operands have *known* values. This expression defines the value of the function call

```
small('p')
```

Programming terminology makes a distinction between the *formal parameter* x in the function definition and the *actual parameter* 'p' in the function designator. The function call replaces an unknown quantity (the formal parameter) by a known value (the actual parameter). This replacement is known as *value substitution*.

It may be helpful to explain these ideas again in slightly more general terms:

The *function definition*

```
static boolean small(char x)
{ return ('a' <= x) & (x <= 'z'); }
```

consists of a heading and a body.

The *function heading* or *signature*

```
static boolean small(char x)
```

defines the *function type* boolean, the *function name* small, and the *formal parameter* x. The formal parameter is a local variable that holds the value of the actual parameter during an invocation of the function. At this point, it is not important (or interesting) to know why Java insists that the heading must include the keyword static.

The *function body*

```
{ return ('a' <= x) & (x <= 'z'); }
```

is a block statement, which, in this case, contains a single statement only

```
return ('a' <= x) & (x <= 'z');
```

This return statement defines the *function value* by means of a boolean expression.

The value of the *function designator*

```
small(ch)
```

is computed in three steps determined by the actual parameter and the function definition:

1. The formal parameter is created as a new variable. This variable is automatically initialized with the value of the actual parameter.

2. The execution of the function body computes and returns the function value.

3. The formal parameter ceases to exist.

4. The program execution continues immediately after the function designator.

Notice that a function is not executed until it is invoked.

In concise terminology, a function designator is a text symbol that *denotes* the invocation of a function. The invocation takes place when a computer *executes* the compiled code of the designator. Now that you are aware of *the important distinction between the static nature of a program text and the dynamic aspects of its execution,* I will sometimes omit this fine point to make this book a little easier to read. It is, after all, a textbook for beginners (and not a language report for professionals).

So, informally, I will say that the function call `capital(ch)` returns the capital letter that corresponds to a small letter `ch`.

The *character function* `capital` is defined below:

```
static char capital(char letter)
{ return (char)(letter - 'a' + 'A'); }
```

The formal parameter is named `letter` to suggest that this function applies to (small) letters only.

9.2.2 The Program "Full Capitalization II"

The revised version of Program 6.3 includes the functions `small` and `capital`. These functions are defined after the `main` block (but are used within that block).

Program 9.1 *Full Capitalization II.*

```
class capitals extends basic
{ public static void main(String param[]) throws Exception
  { input in = new input("poem");
    output out = new output("results");
    while (in.more())
      { char ch = in.read();
        if (small(ch)) out.write(capital(ch));
```

```
        else out.write(ch);
      }
    in.close(); out.close();
  }

  static boolean small(char x)
  { return ('a' <= x) & (x <= 'z'); }

  static char capital(char letter)
  { return (char)(letter - 'a' + 'A'); }
}
```

9.3 SIMPLE PROCEDURES

A *procedure* is a method that defines a computation which does not return
a value.

9.3.1 The Procedure Concept

Program 3.2 asks you to name the author of a novel. I will rewrite this
program by defining a procedure, named `novel`:

```
  static void novel(String title, String author)
    throws Exception
{ input in = new input();
  output out = new output();
  out.writeln("Who wrote the novel \"" + title + "\"?");
  out.writeln("Type the author's full name");
  String answer = in.readline();
  if (answer.equals(author))
    out.writeln(answer + " is correct!");
  else
    out.writeln(answer + " is incorrect. Try again.");
  in.close(); out.close();
}
```

This *procedure definition* consists of a procedure heading and a procedure
body. The *procedure heading* or *signature* consists of

- the *procedure name* `novel`,

- the keyword `void`, which indicates that the procedure does not return
  a value and therefore has no type, and

- the *formal parameters* `title` and `author`.

The *procedure body* is a block statement with three local variables, named `in`, `out`, and `answer`.

An *exception* is an unexpected event that causes abrupt termination of program execution (Flanagan 1996). It may, for example, be caused by an attempt to read past the end of a file. The required clause, `throws Exception`, implies that the procedure `novel` may "throw" an exception, since it uses the input/output methods of the Java text program.

A procedure defines a named operation. The execution of this operation is called a *procedure invocation* or a *procedure call*.

The *procedure statement*

```
novel("The Color Purple", "Alice Walker");
```

denotes an invocation of the procedure `novel`. This procedure statement is equivalent to the following block statement:

```
{ String title = "The Color Purple";
  String author = "Alice Walker";
  input in = new input();
  output out = new output();
  out.writeln("Who wrote the novel \"" + title + "\"?");
  out.writeln("Type the author's full name");
  String answer = in.readline();
  if (answer.equals(author))
    out.writeln(answer + " is correct!");
  else
    out.writeln(answer + " is incorrect. Try again.");
  in.close(); out.close();
}
```

The block statement is a copy of the procedure block in which the formal parameters have been replaced by two local variables. The corresponding actual parameters are initially assigned to these variables (which are unknown outside the block statement).

Here is an alternative explanation that more closely mirrors the computational steps of a procedure call:

1. The formal parameters are created as new variables. These variables are automatically initialized with the values of the corresponding actual parameters.

2. The procedure body is executed. The local variables (if any) are created as new (uninitialized) variables.

3. The formal parameters and the local variables cease to exist.

4. The program execution continues immediately after the procedure statement.

9.3.2   The Program "Authors II"

As you will now realize, the `main` block of a program is just the body of a procedure, named `main`. The revised program therefore consists of two procedures, `novel` and `main`. You can write these procedures in any order you wish. This time, I have placed the `main` procedure after the `novel` procedure.

The whole program is a `class`, which I have defined as "a named group of related methods" (see 1.2.5). The class name `authors` is also the program name.

When you run the compiled program, the computer looks for a procedure, named `main`, and executes the body of this procedure. If you like, the program is executed by invoking its `main` method from the keyboard.

Program 9.2   *Authors II.*

```
class authors extends basic
{ static void novel(String title, String author)
    throws Exception
  { input in = new input();
    output out = new output();
    out.writeln("Who wrote the novel \"" + title + "\"?");
    out.writeln("Type the author's full name");
    String answer = in.readline();
    if (answer.equals(author))
      out.writeln(answer + " is correct!");
    else
      out.writeln(answer + " is incorrect. Try again.");
    in.close(); out.close();
  }

  public static void main(String param[]) throws Exception
  { random chance = new random(1, 5);
    switch (chance.readint())
      { case 1:
          novel("The Bell", "Iris Murdoch");
          break;
        case 2:
          novel("The Color Purple", "Alice Walker");
          break;
        case 3:
          novel("The Golden Notebook", "Dorris Lessing");
          break;
        case 4:
```

```
            novel("Murder on the Orient Express", "Agatha Christie");
            break;
         case 5:
            novel("Ship of Fools", "Katherine Anne Porter");
            break;
      }
      chance.close();
   }
}
```

9.3.3 Value Parameters

So far, I have only discussed methods that use formal *value parameters*. These are local variables that are initialized with the values of actual parameters when a method is invoked.

A method body can change the initial value of a value parameter by assignment. However, since a value parameter is a local variable, it disappears at the end of the invocation, and so does its final value. Consequently, *a value parameter cannot be used to change the value of a variable used as an actual parameter.*

In Java, a formal parameter of a simple type (`boolean`, `char`, `double`, or `int`) is always a value parameter. A formal parameter of type `String` has the same effect as a value parameter, provided the method body does not apply comparison operators to the parameter (see 2.8).

9.4 PARSING METHODS

To apply functions and procedures to a more substantial problem, I will rewrite Program 6.4, which evaluates the readability of an English text.

9.4.1 Syntax Analysis

I will again use *syntax-directed programming* to analyze the input text (see 6.7.4). I will, however, use *methods* (instead of abstract statements) as program pieces.

A complete `Text` consists of one or more sentences followed by an end of file symbol `EOF`:

Text: Sentence { Sentence } EOF

The basic idea of syntax-directed programming is refined as follows:

- *For each syntax rule, define a parsing method with the same name.*

The first parsing method is an integer function, named **Text**. When this function is invoked, it reads a complete text from an input file and computes the average number of words per sentence.

```
static int Text(input in) throws Exception
{ in.readblanks();
  int words = Sentence(in),
    sentences = 1;
  while (in.more())
    { words = words + Sentence(in);
      sentences = sentences + 1;
    }
  return words/sentences;
}
```

The function body uses another parsing method to input a **Sentence** and return its length (in words). The use of the (still unknown) function **Sentence** illustrates another programming rule:

- *To parse a text described by a syntax rule, invoke a method with the same name as the rule.*

The next syntax rule says that a **Sentence** consists of one or more words (possibly separated by commas), followed by an end of sentence mark **EOS**:

```
Sentence: Word { [ , ] Word } EOS
```

The corresponding parsing function inputs and counts one word at a time and skips commas (if any):

```
static int Sentence(input in) throws Exception
  { int words = Word(in);
    while (!EOS(in))
      { if (in.next() == ',')
          { in.readnext(); in.readblanks(); }
        words = words + Word(in);
      }
    in.readnext(); in.readblanks();
    return words;
  }
```

A **Word** consists of one or more **Letter(s)**:

```
Word: Letter { Letter }
```

For the sake of consistency, the corresponding parsing method is a function that returns the number of words it reads (which is always 1):

```
static int Word(input in) throws Exception
{ String name = in.readname();
  in.readblanks();
  return 1;
}
```

An end of sentence symbol EOS is either a colon, a question mark, or a period:

```
EOS: : | ? | .
```

The corresponding parsing function is a boolean function that determines if the next input character is one of the above:

```
static boolean EOS(input in) throws Exception
{ char ch = in.next();
  return (ch == ':') | (ch == '?') | (ch == '.');
}
```

9.4.2 The Program "Readability II"

After combining the parsing methods, I obtain the elegant Program 9.3, in which:

- The main block uses a string function data to return a file name typed by the user.

- Each syntax rule is written as a comment before the corresponding parsing method.

- The input file defined in the main block, and the corresponding method parameters all have the same name in. They are, however, considered different variables, which just happen to have the same name. This is all right, since they are defined in different non-nested blocks (see 7.2.4).

Program 9.3 *Readability Test II.*

```
class readability extends basic
{ public static void main(String param[]) throws Exception
  { input in = new input(data());
    output out = new output("results");
    int length = Text(in);
```

```
    if (length <= 8) out.write("4th grade");
    else if (length <= 11) out.write("5th grade");
    else if (length <= 14) out.write("6th grade");
    else if (length <= 17) out.write("7-8th grade");
    else if (length <= 24) out.write("High school");
    else out.write("College");
    out.writeln(" level: " + length
      + " words per sentence");
    in.close(); out.close();
}

static String data() throws Exception
{ input in = new input();
  output out = new output();
  out.writeln("Type file name");
  String title = in.readword();
  in.close(); out.close();
  return title;
}

/* Text: Sentence { Sentence } EOF */

static int Text(input in) throws Exception
{ in.readblanks();
  int words = Sentence(in),
    sentences = 1;
  while (in.more())
    { words = words + Sentence(in);
      sentences = sentences + 1;
    }
  return words/sentences;
}

/* Sentence: Word { [ , ] Word } EOS */

static int Sentence(input in) throws Exception
{ int words = Word(in);
  while (!EOS(in))
    { if (in.next() == ',')
        { in.readnext(); in.readblanks(); }
      words = words + Word(in);
    }
  in.readnext(); in.readblanks();
  return words;
}

/* Word: Letter { Letter } */

static int Word(input in) throws Exception
{ String name = in.readname();
  in.readblanks();
```

```
    return 1;
  }

  /* EOS: : | ? | . */

  static boolean EOS(input in) throws Exception
  { char ch = in.next();
    return (ch == ':') | (ch == '?') | (ch == '.');
  }
}
```

9.5 ARRAY PARAMETERS

Let me show you how to use methods with array parameters.

9.5.1 Simple Array Parameters

Program 7.1 uses a `boolean` array to keep track of m random reservations in a hotel with n rooms. Procedures can be used to divide the `main` block of this program into procedure statements with readable names:

```
{ output out = new output("results");
  int m = 8 /* guests */, n = 10 /* rooms */;
  boolean free[] = new boolean[n+1];
  initialize(free, n);
  reserve(free, n, m);
  list(free, n, out);
  find(free, n, out);
  out.close();
}
```

The hotel is `initialized` with n free rooms:

```
static void initialize(boolean free[], int n)
{ for (int i = 1; i <= n; i++) free[i] = true; }
```

The *formal parameter* definition

```
boolean free[]
```

does *not* include the array length. Consequently, the procedure can be applied to a `boolean` array of any length. However, the `for` statement must somehow be able to determine the length of the actual array parameter. In this case, the number of elements *used* is defined by another formal parameter n.

9.5.2 Reference Parameters

The main and initialize methods both define a local array variable, named free. These are different variables defined in different methods. I will (temporarily) rename the variables in initialize to be able to tell them apart from the variables in main:

```
static void initialize(boolean vacant[], int last)
{ for (int k = 1; k <= last; k++) vacant[k] = true; }
```

The procedure call

```
initialize(free, n);
```

is intended to be equivalent to executing the following block statement in the main method:

```
{ for (int k = 1; k <= n; k++) free[k] = true; }
```

This block statement is a copy of the procedure block in which every occurrence of the formal parameters, variant and last, have been replaced by the corresponding actual parameters free and n.

The formal parameter n is a value parameter. However, since the purpose of the procedure is to *change* the elements of the actual parameter free, the formal parameter vacant cannot be a value parameter (see 9.3.3).

The procedure call is intended to perform exactly the same operations on the actual array parameter as the body performs on the formal array parameter. As an example, the assignment

```
vacant[k] = true;
```

of the value true to the kth element of the array vacant stands for assigning the same value to the kth element of the array free

```
free[k] = true;
```

In other words, the formal parameter name vacant is just a local name for the actual parameter free. If you like, every occurrence of the name vacant in the body really *refers* to the array free. This kind of formal parameter is known as a *reference parameter*. The conceptual replacement of a reference parameter by an actual array parameter is called *reference substitution*. During an invocation of the method, the reference parameter is said to be *bound* to the corresponding actual parameter.

In Java, any formal parameter that is not a value parameter is a reference parameter. Consequently, *all array parameters are reference parameters.*

9.5.3   The Program "Hotel Rooms II"

The procedure `reserve` uses a local `random` number generator to simulate the arrival of m guests. The procedures `list` and `find` are very similar.

Program 9.4 *Hotel Rooms II.*

```
class rooms extends basic
{ public static void main(String param[]) throws Exception
  { int m = 8 /* guests */, n = 10 /* rooms */;
    output out = new output("results");
    boolean free[] = new boolean[n+1];
    initialize(free, n);
    reserve(free, n, m);
    list(free, n, out);
    find(free, n, out);
    out.close();
  }

  static void initialize(boolean free[], int n)
  { for (int i = 1; i <= n; i++) free[i] = true; }

  static void reserve(boolean free[], int n, int m)
    throws Exception
  { random choice = new random(1, n);
    for (int i = 1; i <= m; i++)
      free[choice.readint()] = false;
  }

  static void list(boolean free[], int n, output out)
    throws Exception
  { for (int i = 1; i <= n; i++)
      if (free[i]) out.writeln("Room " + i + " is free");
    out.writeln();
  }

  static void find(boolean free[], int n, output out)
    throws Exception
  { int i = 1, j = n;
    while (i < j)
      if (free[i]) j = i;
      else i = i + 1;
    if (free[i]) out.writeln("Room " + i + " is free");
    else out.writeln("There is no free room");
  }
}
```

9.6   SCOPE RULES OF METHODS

Classes and methods serve the same purpose as blocks: they *localize* the use of some definitions in a program. I will refer to the bodies of these units as *class blocks* and *method blocks*.

Program 9.4 includes five method definitions:

```
class rooms ...
{ public static void main(...) ...
  { ... }

  static void initialize(...)
  { ... }

  static void reserve(...) ...
  { ... }

  static void list(...) ...
  { ... }

  static void find(...) ...
  { ... }
}
```

Sadly enough, the scope rules for methods and variables are similar, but not quite the same (see 5.3.1). I will simplify these rules by ignoring certain complications:

- *All methods defined in the same class must normally have different names.*

- *A method defined in a class is known throughout the class.*

Consequently, the methods can be defined in any order, and any method can call any other method. In Program 9.4, the `main` method (defined at the beginning) calls the `find` method (defined at the end):

```
class rooms ...
{ public static void main(...)
  { ... find(...); ... }
  ...
  static void find(...)
  { ... }
}
```

Notice that `find` is *local* to the `class`, but is *global* to the body of the `main` method (see 5.3.2).

In the `find` method

```
static void find(boolean free[], int n, output out) throws Exception
{ int i = 1, j = n;
  while (i < j)
    if (free[i]) j = i;
    else i = i + 1;
  if (free[i]) out.writeln("Room " + i + " is free");
  else out.writeln("There is no free room");
}
```

the *formal parameters* free, n, and out, as well as the variables i and j, are *local variables* of the method.

- A formal parameter defined in a method is known from its definition in the method heading to the end of the method body.

9.7 ARRAY FUNCTIONS

I will rewrite Program 8.1 to illustrate functions that compute and return complete matrices.

9.7.1 Global Variables

In Program 9.4, each procedure includes a formal parameter n that defines the number of elements used in a simple array. In the spreadsheet program, I will take another approach and define the number of rows and columns used at the beginning of the program:

```
class spreadsheet extends basic
{ static int m = 11 /* rows */, n = 5 /* columns */;

  public static void main(String param[]) throws Exception
  { ... }

  static int[][] readsheet(input in)
    throws Exception
  { int table[][] = new int[m+1][n+1];
    ...
  }

  ...
}
```

The variables m and n are defined in a block (the class spreadsheet) that contains all other blocks (including the main block and the function shown). Since m and n are *global* to all methods in the program, they are accessible throughout the program (see 5.3.2).

9.7.2   Matrix Functions and Parameters

The function `readsheet` inputs the `spreadsheet` data in a local matrix, named `table`, and returns the whole matrix as the function value:

```
static int[][] readsheet(input in)
  throws Exception
{ int table[][] = new int[m+1][n+1];
  for (int i = 1; i <= m - 1; i++)
    for (int j = 1; j <= n - 1; j++)
      table[i][j] = in.readint();
  return table;
}
```

The function `rowsum` uses a formal matrix parameter, named `table`, to compute the sum of all elements in row number `i` with column numbers from `first` to `last`:

```
static int rowsum(int table[][], int i,
  int first, int last)
{ int sum = 0;
  for (int j = first; j <= last; j++)
    sum = sum + table[i][j];
  return sum;
}
```

In short, the function computes the sum

```
table[i][first] + table[i][first+1] + ... + table[i][last]
```

assuming that $1 \leq$ `i` $\leq$ `m`, and $1 \leq$ `first` $\leq$ `last` $\leq$ `n`.

9.7.3   The Program "Spreadsheet II"

The rest of the `spreadsheet` program should now be easy to understand.

Program 9.5 *Spreadsheet II.*

```
class spreadsheet extends basic
{ static int m = 11 /* rows */, n = 5 /* columns */;

  public static void main(String param[]) throws Exception
  { input in = new input("spreadsheet");
    output out = new output("results");
    int table[][] = readsheet(in);
    for (int i = 1; i <= m - 1; i++)
      table[i][n] = rowsum(table, i, 3, n - 1);
    for (int j = 2; j <= n; j++)
      table[m][j] = columnsum(table, j, 1, m - 1);
```

```
    writesheet(out, table);
    in.close(); out.close();
}

static int[][] readsheet(input in)
  throws Exception
{ int table[][] = new int[m+1][n+1];
  for (int i = 1; i <= m - 1; i++)
    for (int j = 1; j <= n - 1; j++)
      table[i][j] = in.readint();
  return table;
}

static int rowsum(int table[][], int i,
  int first, int last)
{ int sum = 0;
  for (int j = first; j <= last; j++)
    sum = sum + table[i][j];
  return sum;
}

static int columnsum(int table[][], int j,
  int first, int last)
{ int sum = 0;
  for (int i = first; i <= last; i++)
    sum = sum + table[i][j];
  return sum;
}

static void writesheet(output out, int table[][])
  throws Exception
{ out.writeln("        YEAR      MILES" +
    "   OPERATING  OWNING     TOTAL");
  out.writeln("                          DRIVEN" +
    "    COSTS     COSTS     COSTS");
  out.writeln();
  int i, j, width = 10;
  for (i = 1; i <= m - 1; i++)
    { for (j = 1; j <= n; j++)
        out.write(table[i][j], width);
      out.writeln();
    }
  out.writeln("   -------    ------" +
    "    ----     -----     -----");
  out.write("    1979-88");
  for (j = 2; j <= n; j++)
    out.write(table[m][j], width);
  out.writeln();
  }
}
```

9.8   ABSTRACTION

Abstraction is our mental ability to concentrate on those aspects of the world that we consider essential at the moment, and ignore those details that seem less important. Abstraction is a form of *selective ignorance* that enables you to concentrate on one thing at a time.

A method is a perfect example of abstraction: when you program a method, you must carefully consider *how* the method works in detail. However, when you use the method, you can ignore these details and concentrate on understanding *what* the method does as a whole.

This view of abstraction is also reflected in my dictionary, which includes the definition: "*abstract*, something that concentrates in itself the essential qualities of anything more extensive or more general, or of several things."

However, the dictionary fails to convey the important point that what is considered essential in one context may be unimportant in another. Abstraction is a mental mechanism for *focusing on a simplified view* of the world that serves our purpose at the moment. But, if we change our perspective from, say, using a method to inventing it, the focus of interest naturally changes. In short, what is considered essential depends on your current focus of interest.

I am therefore convinced that my dictionary is misleading when it also defines *abstract* as "theoretical; not applied or practical." Abstraction is just another word for *divide and conquer*—the only way we know how to deal with problems that are too complicated to be grasped at once.

9.9   ADVANTAGES OF METHODS

In the hands of a skilled programmer, the method concept is a powerful thinking tool that can simplify a program in several ways:

- Methods partition a program into *self-contained subprograms* that can be written, tested, described, and understood, one at a time.

- Methods *localize assumptions* about the use of related variables and statements. This makes it easier to replace an incorrect or slow method by a better method without changing the rest of the program.

- Method names introduce *terminology* for describing and understanding a program.

- Method names can *shorten* a program text if the same method is used in several places. However, methods can also help you understand a program, even if they are only used once.

These advantages are just different aspects of *abstraction*.

Finally, method invocation supports *efficient memory utilization* by releasing memory occupied by local variables when it is no longer needed, so it can be reused for other variables.

9.10   JAVA PITFALLS

My explanation of *array parameters* is only correct if you impose the following restrictions on your use of this concept. Any program that violates these restrictions can have unexpected results, which are not detected during compilation or execution.

- **Do not use the assignment operator for array parameters.**

Example:

```
static void copy(boolean vacant[], boolean free[])
{ vacant = free; }
```

Remedy: see 7.3.

- **Do not use comparison operators for array parameters.**

Example:

```
static boolean equal(boolean free[], boolean vacant[])
{ return free == vacant; }
```

Remedy: see 7.3.

- **Do not return array parameters.**

Example:

```
static boolean[] copy(boolean free[])
{ return free; }
```

Instead, copy the array parameter into a local array variable (see 7.3) and return the local array value:

```
static boolean[] copy(boolean free[], int n)
{ boolean clone[] = new boolean[n+1];
  for (int i = 1; i <= n; i++) clone[i] = free[i];
  return clone;
}
```

- **Do not use actual array parameters unless they are distinct.**

Example:

```
static void initialize(boolean vacant[], boolean used[], int n)
{ for (int i = 1; i <= n; i++)
    { vacant[i] = true; used[i] = false; }
}
```

The purpose of this simple procedure is obviously to set all the elements of two *distinct arrays* to true and false, respectively. However, in the procedure call

```
initialize(free, free, n);
```

the same array variable free occurs twice as an actual parameter. In this case, the formal parameters, vacant and used, are *aliases* for the *same array*. Since the elements of the array free cannot be true and false at the same time, we must conclude that even the most "obvious" understanding of a method becomes invalid in the presence of aliasing.

Remedy: rewrite the program without using aliasing.

9.11   PROGRAMMING EXERCISES

Exercise 9.1 Silly Jeopardy II

Write a Java program for Exercise 1.3. Your program must include the following procedure:

```
public void ask(input in, output out, String answer,
    String question) throws Exception
```

The procedure outputs a given answer, inputs the user's guess, contradicts the user, and outputs a given question. The following example illustrates the use of this procedure:

```
ask(in, out, "An anchor",
    "What\'s tattooed on Popeye\'s arm?");
```

Exercise 9.2 U.S. Geography II

Write a Java program for Exercise 2.2. Your program must include the following function:

```
static int points(input in, output out, String question,
  String answer) throws Exception
```

The function outputs a given question, inputs the user's guess, and tells the user whether or not it is identical to a given answer. The function value is 1 for a correct answer and 0 for an incorrect one. The following example illustrates the use of this function.

```
correct = correct +
  points(in, out, "What state gets the most rain",
    "Hawaii");
```

Exercise 9.3 Tomorrow's Date II

Write a Java program that solves Exercise 3.1. Your program must include the following functions and procedures:

```
static int lastday(int month, int year)
```

The value is the number of days in a given month in a given year.

```
static boolean valid(int day, int month, int day)
```

The value is true if a given date exists, and false if it does not.

```
static void writenext(output out, int day,
  int month, int year) throws Exception
```

Uses a given date to compute and output tomorrow's date.

Exercise 9.4 The Odds of Craps

Write a Java program that computes the odds of winning the game of craps by simulating 10000 games and displaying the number of games won. You may use pieces of your earlier program that plays a single game of craps, but do *not* display the outcomes of individual throws and games (see Exercise 5.2). Your program must include the following functions and procedures:

```
static int roll(random die1, random die2)
```

Rolls two dice once and returns an integer between 2 and 12.

```
static boolean win(random die1, random die2)
```

Plays a single game of craps and returns the boolean value true, if the game was won, and false, if it was lost.

```
static void play(int games, output out)
```

Plays a given number of games and writes the number of games won in a given output file.

Exercise 9.5 Find Pangrams II

Write a Java program for Exercise 7.2. Your program must include a function that reads a sentence and returns an array defining how many times each letter of the alphabet occurs in the sentence, and another function that determines if the sentence is a pangram by examining the array of letters.

Exercise 9.6 Magic Squares II

Write a Java program that solves Exercise 8.1. Your program must include the following functions and procedures that operate on a square matrix with n×n integers:

```
static int[][] readmatrix(input in) throws Exception
```

The value is a square matrix input from a given file.

```
static void writematrix(output out, int square[][])
   throws Exception
```

Outputs a square matrix to a given file.

```
static int diagonal1(int square[][])
```

The value is the sum of the elements of one of the diagonals of a square matrix.

```
static int diagonal2(int square[][])
```

The value is the sum of the elements of the other diagonal of a square matrix.

```
static int row(int square[][], int i)
```

The value is the sum of the elements of the ith row of a square matrix.

```
static int column(int square[][], int j)
```

The value is the sum of the elements of the jth column of a square matrix.

The dimension n is a global program constant:

```
static int = 4;
```

Exercise 9.7 The Game of Life II

Write a Java program that solves Exercise 8.2. Your program must include two functions that initialize and update the board, and a procedure that displays the board.

10

RECURSION

This chapter introduces *recursion*, one of the most beautiful ideas in computer programming. (You may skip this chapter on a first reading and return to it later.)

10.1 RECURSIVE METHODS

A method is recursive if it calls itself. At first, you may find this idea mindblowing. But you will soon discover that recursion is a natural and elegant programming concept for some problems.

10.1.1 Recursive Definitions

In how many different ways can you select two out of three playing cards? Well, if you number the three cards

```
1 2 3
```

it is not too hard to see that you can select a pair of cards in three different ways:

```
1 2
1 3
2 3
```

However, since this book is about programming, I would like to use a function call

```
ways(2,3)
```

to compute the number of ways of choosing two out of three cards.

Here I have to add a touch of mathematics (but nothing obtrusive). If you look at the three different ways of picking two cards, they fall into two groups: the two pairs that include the third card, and the one that doesn't.

If you always pick the third card, then you can get the same pairs

```
1 3
2 3
```

by picking one of the first two cards

```
1
2
```

and adding the third card to each pair. Since you can only pick one of two cards in two different ways, it means that

```
ways(1,2) = 2
```

On the other hand, if you don't pick the third card, then your only choice is to pick the first two cards

```
1 2
```

which can only be done in one way. In other words,

```
ways(2,2) = 1
```

Now, the original three pairs consist of those that include the third card plus the one that doesn't. Consequently,

```
ways(2,3) = ways(1,2) + ways(2,2) = 2 + 1 = 3
```

Suppose you have n (instead of 3) cards. Then you can select one of these cards in n different ways:

```
ways(1,n) = n
```

Needless to say, there is only one way to select all the cards:

```
ways(n,n) = 1
```

In general, I am interested in computing the number of ways in which you can select m out of n cards:

```
ways(m,n)
```

If you always pick the nth card, you can obtain the same hands by picking m-1 of the first n-1 cards and adding the nth card to each hand. The number of ways in which you can do this is (by definition)

```
ways(m-1,n-1)
```

But if you don't pick the nth card, you must choose m out of the remaining n−1 cards. In that case, the number of different ways is

```
ways(m,n-1)
```

Since the original hands consist of those that include the nth card and those that don't, we now know that

```
ways(m,n) = ways(m-1,n-1) + ways(m,n-1)
```

In mathematics, a *recursive definition* of a function is one in which the first few cases are given and the general case is defined in terms of one or more previous cases. The problem of choosing m out of n cards is defined by three recursive rules:

```
Rule 1: ways(m,n) = 1  if m = n

Rule 2: ways(m,n) = n  if m = 1

Rule 3: ways(m,n) = ways(m-1,n-1) + ways(m,n-1)  if 1 < m < n
```

To calculate, say, the number of ways in which you can choose 2 out of 4 cards, use Rule 3 to split the problem into two evaluations of the same function with smaller parameter values:

```
ways(2,4) = ways(1,3) + ways(2,3)
```

Rule 2 immediately tells you that

```
ways(1,3) = 3
```

The second subproblem can itself be broken down into two function evaluations with still smaller parameter values:

```
ways(2,3) = ways(1,2) + ways(2,2)
```

This *divide and conquer* process terminates when it reaches the point where the function value is defined either by Rule 2:

```
ways(1,2) = 2
```

or by Rule 1:

```
ways(2,2) = 1
```

You can now go back through the list of function evaluations and add the previous results (according to Rule 3):

```
ways(2,3) = ways(1,2) + ways(2,2) = 2 + 1 = 3
```

until you have calculated the function value for the original parameter values:

```
ways(2,4) = ways(1,3) + ways(2,3) = 3 + 3 = 6
```

In short, you can select two out of four cards in six different ways:

```
1 2
1 3
1 4
2 3
2 4
3 4
```

For small parameter values, you may be able to evaluate a recursive function by paper and pencil. However, if you want to know in how many different ways you can select and play 5 out of 100 compact discs, you will need a computer to discover that

```
ways(5,100) = 75,287,520
```

10.1.2   Recursive Invocations

The recursive definition of the function **ways** can be used almost verbatim to write a *recursive function* in Java:

```java
static int ways(int m, int n)
{ int number;
   if (m == n) number = 1;
   else if (m == 1) number = n;
   else number = ways(m - 1, n - 1) + ways(m, n - 1);
   return number;
}
```

Here's what happens when a program calls this function to evaluate

```
ways(2,3)
```

The function call creates fresh copies of the formal value parameters, and initializes these instances of m and n, with the actual parameter values 2 and 3. In the following, I will simply refer to this invocation as ways(2,3). When this execution of the function body reaches the expression

```
ways(m-1,n-1) + ways(m,n-1)
```

the function invokes itself to evaluate the first term

```
ways(m-1,n-1)
```

In this case, this is equivalent to the function call

```
ways(1,2)
```

There are now two incomplete function invocations in progress:

```
ways(2,3) ways(1,2)
```

The first invocation, ways(2,3), cannot continue until the second invocation, ways(1,2), has returned a value.

Now, ways(1,2) also creates fresh copies of the formal parameters and assigns the values 1 and 2 to these variable instances. Since this m is equal to 1, ways(1,2) returns the value of n, which is 2. This completes ways(1,2), and the corresponding parameter instances cease to exist.

The only activation still in progress

```
ways(2,3)
```

continues its execution at the point where the function body calls the function again to evaluate the second term

```
ways(m,n-1)
```

that is, ways(2,2).

The list of incomplete function calls now looks like this

```
ways(2,3) ways(2,2)
```

Like any other invocation, ways(2,2) creates fresh parameter instances, this time with the values 2 and 2. Since both parameters have the same value, ways(2,2) returns the function value 1 to ways(2,3).

The remaining invocation

```
ways(2,3)
```

uses the previous function results to complete the addition

```
ways(m-1,n-1) + ways(m,n-1) = ways(1,2) + ways(2,2)
                             = 2 + 1
                             = 3
```

and returns 3 as the value of `ways(2,3)`.

10.1.3   Invocation Traces

The recursive computation is summarized by the following *invocation trace*:

```
ways(2,3) ways(1,2) return 2
ways(2,3)
ways(2,3) ways(2,2) return 1
ways(2,3)
ways(2,3) return 3
```

Each line is a list of incomplete invocations in progress. A return value marks the termination of an invocation. After each return, the remaining previous invocations are listed on a new line.

The invocation trace for the computation of `ways(2,4)` looks like this:

```
ways(2,4) ways(1,3) return 3
ways(2,4)
ways(2,4) ways(2,3) ways(1,2) return 2
ways(2,3) ways(2,3)
ways(2,3) ways(2,3) ways(2,2) return 1
ways(2,3) ways(2,3)
ways(2,3) ways(2,3) return 3
ways(2,4)
ways(2,4) return 6
```

For larger parameter values, the size of the trace grows rapidly. For example:

```
ways(3,5) ways(2,4) ways(1,3) return 3
ways(2,4) ways(2,4)
ways(2,4) ways(2,4) ways(2,3) ways(1,2) return 2
ways(2,3) ways(2,3) ways(2,3)
ways(2,3) ways(2,3) ways(2,3) ways(2,2) return 1
ways(2,3) ways(2,3) ways(2,3)
ways(2,3) ways(2,3) ways(2,3) return 3
ways(2,4) ways(2,4)
ways(2,4) ways(2,4) return 6
ways(3,5)
ways(3,5) ways(3,4) ways(2,3) ways(1,2) return 2
ways(2,3) ways(2,3) ways(2,3)
ways(2,3) ways(2,3) ways(2,3) ways(2,2) return 1
ways(2,3) ways(2,3) ways(2,3)
ways(2,3) ways(2,3) ways(2,3) return 3
ways(3,4) ways(3,4)
ways(3,4) ways(3,4) ways(3,3) return 1
```

```
ways(3,4) ways(3,4)
ways(3,4) ways(3,4) return 4
ways(3,5)
ways(3,5) return 10
```

This trace shows that the same function values are computed over and over again. Consequently, this particular method is an *inefficient* way of computing the function values `ways(m,n)`. Incidentally, these values play an important role in probability theory, where they are known as *binomial coefficients* (Weaver 1963).

10.1.4   Variable Definitions and Instances

To understand recursion, you must make a sharp distinction between two different meanings of the word *variable*:

- A *variable definition* is a symbol in the program text. The *scope* of a variable is a property of the program text: it refers to that part of the program text in which the variable name can be used.

- A *variable instance* is a memory location that holds an incarnation of the variable during program execution. The *duration* of a variable instance is a property of the program execution: each variable instance exists during a particular invocation only.

To illustrate this important distinction, I will use a more detailed *invocation trace* of a recursive function call.

To compute `ways(3,5)`, the function initially calls itself twice. Each invocation creates fresh instances of the value parameters `m` and `n` and the local variable `number`. The third invocation `ways(1,3)` returns the value 3 to the second invocation `ways(2,4)`:

Instance	1	2	3
m	3	2	1
n	5	4	3
number	?	?	3

At this point, the third instances of the variables cease to exist.

The function now calls itself twice again, creating the fourth and fifth instances of the same variables:

Instance	1	2	4	5
m	3	2	2	1
n	5	4	3	2
number	?	?	?	2

When `ways(1,2)` returns the value 2, the fifth instances cease to exist.

The fourth invocation, `ways(2,3)`, then returns the value 3 to the second invocation `ways(2,4)`:

Instance	1	2	4
m	3	2	2
n	5	4	3
number	?	?	3

and so on.

Since recursive invocation creates multiple instances of the same variables, it raises a question: when the program text refers to a variable by its name, which instance of the variable are we talking about? The answer is that *a variable name always refers to the most recent instance of the variable that still exists.* In the previous invocation traces, a variable name always denotes the corresponding instance in the rightmost column.

When an invocation ends and the most recent variable instances cease to exist, the variable names denote the previous instances of the same variables, and so on. Finally, when the initial invocation has returned a result, all variable instances created (directly or indirectly) by this call have disappeared.

Notice that function invocations terminate (and their variable instances disappear) in *last-in, first-out* order.

There is no difference between a single invocation of a recursive and a non-recursive function: in both cases, an invocation creates fresh instances of the formal parameters and local variables, which last until the invocation ends. However, since a non-recursive function does not call itself, there is never more than one instance of its variables in existence at a time. In this special case, it is easy to forget the distinction between a variable definition and a variable instance. Nevertheless, it is important to remember that the local variable instances also disappear at the end of a non-recursive function call. The next time you call the same function, the previous values of its local variables no longer exist. Instead, you have fresh uninitialized instances of the same variables.

10.1.5 Termination of Recursion

When you first learn about recursion, it seems less mysterious if you understand how recursive invocations take place. But once you know that, it is easier to ignore the *dynamic details* of recursion and check that the program text has the following *static properties*:

- The function corresponds directly to the recursive rules that define its values.

- When the function invokes itself recursively at least one of its parameter values is reduced (and none of them are increased).

- For sufficiently small parameter values, a function call returns a value and terminates.

Similar rules apply if a function calls itself with increased parameter values until some upper limit is reached.

If a recursive function has these characteristics, it will return a value within a finite time (unless its initial actual parameters are meaningless). You can therefore ignore the minute details of recursive invocations.

10.1.6 The Program "Choose Cards"

Program 10.1 uses the recursive function to compute the number of different ways in which you can choose a hand of m cards from a deck of n cards.

Program 10.1 *Choose Cards.*

```
/* Computes the number of ways in which you can choose m
   out of n playing cards using the following recursive
   rules:

   ways(m,n) = 1  for m = n
   ways(m,n) = n  for m = 1
   ways(m,n) = ways(m-1,n-1) + ways(m,n-1)  for 1 < m < n
*/

class choose extends basic
{ static int ways(int m, int n)
   { int number;
```

```
         if (m == n) number = 1;
         else if (m == 1) number = n;
         else number = ways(m - 1, n - 1) + ways(m, n - 1);
         return number;
      }

   public static void main(String param[]) throws Exception
   { input in = new input();
      output out = new output("results");
      out.writeln("Type m and n");
      int m = in.readint();
      int n = in.readint();
      assume ((1 <= m) & (m <= n));
      out.writeln(ways(m, n));
      in.close(); out.close();
   }
}
```

10.2   MUTUAL RECURSION

10.2.1   Simple Expressions

Here is a nice problem: Program a *calculator* that can add and subtract
natural numbers. It should be able to input and evaluate expressions, such
as

```
11
10 + 2
18 - 5
1 - 12 + 25
```

and output the results

```
11
12
13
14
```

Since the number of possible expressions is endless, it is not sufficient to
characterize the input of the calculator by a few randomly chosen examples.
We must define the syntax of *all possible expressions* by a *grammar* (see 6.7):

```
1.   Expression: Term { Operator Term }
2.   Operator: + | -
3.   Term: Number
4.   Number: Digit { Digit }
```

These syntax rules can be read as follows:

1. An `Expression` consists of a one or more `Terms` separated by `Operators`.

2. An `Operator` is a + or − sign.

3. A `Term` is a `Number`.

4. A `Number` consists of one or more `Digits`.

Any `Operator` or `Number` may be preceded and followed by one or more blanks.

Some of these syntax rules refer to other syntax rules. But no syntax rule refers to itself. It is a *non-recursive grammar*.

10.2.2 Non-Recursive Parsing

With an input grammar in hand, the familiar parsing methods can be seen looming over the horizon (see 9.4). The obvious thing to do is to write a method that inputs and evaluates an `Expression`:

```
/* Expression: Term { Operator Term }
   Operator: + | -
*/

static int Expression(input in) throws Exception
{ int value = Term(in);
  while ((in.next() == '+') | (in.next() == '-'))
    { char ch = in.read();
      if (ch == '+') value = value + Term(in);
      else value = value - Term(in);
    }
  return value;
  }
}
```

The method begins by obtaining the value of the first `Term`. It then proceeds to add or subtract the values of the remaining `Terms` (if any). The function returns the final result of this calculation.

The `Term` method inputs and returns a natural `Number`. The method skips blanks (if any) before and after the `Number`:

```
/* Term: Number
   Number: Digit { Digit }
*/

static int Term(input in) throws Exception
{ in.readblanks();
```

```
    int value = in.readint();
    in.readblanks();
    return value;
}
```

Since the input grammar is non-recursive, the corresponding parsing methods are also non-recursive.

The following *invocation trace* illustrates how these methods work when they parse and evaluate the expression 1 - 12 + 25:

```
expr term return 1
expr
expr term return 12
expr
expr term return 25
expr
expr return 14
```

Since the parsing methods are non-recursive, each of them can only be in the middle of one invocation at a time (or none):

- First, the `Expression` method calls the `Term` method, which returns the `Number` 1.

- `Expression` then activates `Term` again, which yields the `Number` 12.

- After subtracting 12 from 1, `Expression` uses `Term` again to get the `Number` 25, which is subtracted from the previous result to obtain the final value 15.

So far so good.

10.2.3   Recursive Parsing

It makes a dramatic difference if the calculator must handle *subexpressions* enclosed in parentheses. For example:

```
(2 + 15) - ((1 - 3) + 4)
```

Expressions of this form are defined by a *recursive grammar*:

```
1.   Expression: Term { Operator Term }
2.   Operator: + | -
3.   Term: Number | ( Expression )
4.   Number: Digit { Digit }
```

The essential property of this grammar is that an **Expression** consists of **Terms**, which, in turn, may include **Expressions**, and so on. These syntax rules do not refer *directly* to themselves. They do, however, refer *indirectly* to themselves. This is known as *mutual recursion*.

The only rule that has changed is Rule 3, which now specifies that a **Term** can be a parenthesized **Expression**. I will use the revised rule to rewrite the **Term** method in a straightforward manner (as if it were non-recursive):

```
/* Term: Number | ( Expression )
   Number: Digit { Digit }
*/

static int Term(input in) throws Exception
{ int value;
  in.readblanks();
  if (in.digit())
    value = in.readint();
  else
    { char ch = in.read();
      assume(ch == '(');
      value = Expression(in);
      in.readblanks();
      ch = in.read();
      assume(ch == ')');
    }
  in.readblanks();
  return value;
}
```

The evaluation of the expression (2 + 15) - ((1 - 3) + 4) is traced below (with line numbers added):

```
 1.  expr term expr term return 2
 2.  expr term expr
 3.  expr term expr term return 15
 4.  expr term expr
 5.  expr term expr return 17
 6.  expr term
 7.  expr term return 17
 8.  expr
 9.  expr term expr term expr term return 1
10.  expr term expr term expr
11.  expr term expr term expr term return 3
12.  expr term expr term expr
13.  expr term expr term expr return -2
14.  expr term expr term
15.  expr term expr term return -2
16.  expr term expr
17.  expr term expr term return 4
18.  expr term expr
19.  expr term expr return 2
```

```
20.   expr term
21.   expr term return 2
22.   expr
23.   expr return 15
```

Line 9 shows an impressive example of mutual recursion, which involves six incomplete invocations.

10.2.4   The Program "Recursive Calculator"

Program 10.2 evaluates one or more expressions input from a text file.

Program 10.2 *Recursive Calculator.*

```
/* Parses and evaluates integer expressions
   input from a text file.

   Text: Expression { Expression} EOF
   Expression: Term { Operator Term }
   Operator: + | -
   Term: Number | ( Expression )
   Number: Digit { Digit }
*/

class calculator extends basic
{ static int Term(input in) throws Exception
  { int value;
    in.readblanks();
    if (in.digit())
      value = in.readint();
    else
      { char ch = in.read();
        assume(ch == '(');
        value = Expression(in);
        in.readblanks();
        ch = in.read();
        assume(ch == ')');
      }
    in.readblanks();
    return value;
  }

  static int Expression(input in) throws Exception
  { int value = Term(in);
    while ((in.next() == '+') | (in.next() == '-'))
      { char ch = in.read();
        if (ch == '+') value = value + Term(in);
        else value = value - Term(in);
      }
    return value;
```

```
    }

    static void Text(input in, output out) throws Exception
    { out.writeln(Expression(in));
      while (in.more())
        out.writeln(Expression(in));
    }

    public static void main(String param[]) throws Exception
    { input in = new input("expressions");
      output out = new output("results");
      Text(in, out);
      in.close(); out.close();
    }
}
```

10.3 PROGRAMMING EXERCISES

Exercise 10.1 Rabbits II

Write a Java program that solves Exercise 4.5 with the following modification: Your program must include a recursive function

```
static int females(int n)
```

that returns the number of female rabbits after n months.

Exercise 10.2 Reverse Lines

Write a Java program that reads one line at a time and prints all characters (except newline) in reverse order. As an example, the mysterious line

```
sdren fo egnever etamitlu eht si gnimmargorP
```

should be output as

```
Programming is the ultimate revenge of nerds
```

You may not use arrays or strings for this exercise. Hint: use a *recursive procedure* that inputs a single character in a local variable before calling itself to input the next character of the current line.

Use the following input text to test the program:

```
ABLE WAS I ERE I SAW ELBA
WAS IT A BAR OR A BAT I SAW
NORMA IS AS SELFLESS AS I AM RON
```

Exercise 10.3 Coin Change

Write a Java program that outputs the number of possible ways to pay $1 in half-dollars, quarters, dimes, nickels, and pennies. Solve the problem by means of a recursive function

```
static int change(int n, int c)
```

that computes the number of different ways to pay `n` cents, using coins of `c` cents (or less), where c = 50, 25, 10, 5, or 1.

Hint: by definition, 100 cents can be changed in `change(100,50)` ways, using half-dollars (and smaller coins).

1. If at least one half-dollar is used, the remaining 50 cents can also be paid in half-dollars (or smaller coins). This can be done in `change(50,50)` ways.

2. If no half-dollars are used, the 100 cents can only be paid in quarters (or smaller coins). This can be done in `change(100,25)` ways.

For half-dollars, these are the only two possibilities: they are either used, or they are not. So, the total number of ways to change $1 must be the sum of the number of possible ways with and without half-dollar coins:

```
change(100,50) = change(100-50,50) + change(100,25)
```

Exercise 10.4 Choose Cards II

Extend Program 10.1 with statements and methods that output an *invocation trace* of the recursive function `ways` (see 10.1). Use the function call `ways(3,5)` as a test case.

Hint: use arrays of size 100 to keep track of the actual parameters of all incomplete function invocations.

Exercise 10.5 Recursive Calculator II

Rewrite Program 10.2 to evaluate expressions with the following extended syntax:

```
Expression: Term { AddingOperator Term }
AddingOperator: + | -
Term: Factor { MultiplyingOperator Factor }
MultiplyingOperator: * | /
Factor: Number | ( Expression )
Number: Digit { Digit }
```

Use the following expressions as test cases:

```
10 + 2
18 - 5
1 - 12 + 25
(2 + 15) - ((1 - 3) + 4)
(7*(1 + 2) - 3)/6 + 13
```

11

CLASSES

This chapter introduces the *class* concept, which combines related variables and methods into a single program module.

11.1 THE CLASS CONCEPT

This is the moment you have been waiting for: we finally got around to *object-oriented programming*. You have, of course, been using this concept all along to access text files. However, you may not necessarily have studied the input/output classes, which are hidden inside my Java text program. Now you will learn to define classes in your own programs.

My starting point is the program `hangman` which inputs the (hidden) solution to a crossword puzzle, which you must then attempt to guess, one letter at a time.

The following program outline includes the essential details of the main loop of Program 8.2:

```
{ ...
  char a[][] = new char[n+1][n+1];
  char b[][] = new char[n+1][n+1];
  ...
  int known = 0;
  while ((known < n*n) & ...)
    { ...
      char ch = in.read();
      known = 0;
      for (int i = 1; i <= n; i++)
        { for (int j = 1; j <= n; j++)
```

```
            { if (a[i][j] == ch) b[i][j] = ch;
              if (b[i][j] != '?') known = known + 1;
              out.write(b[i][j] + " ");
            }
          out.writeln();
        }
      out.writeln();
      guesses = guesses + 1;
    }
    ...
}
```

The program keeps the complete and partial solutions in two character matrices, a and b. Every time you type a character, the program scans the complete solution and updates the partial solution.

What's wrong with this? Well, it is not so obvious that the body of the while statement performs three distinct tasks:

- Every occurrence (if any) of the typed character is included in the partial solution.

- The updated partial solution is displayed.

- The known characters in the partial solution are counted.

All the programming details of these tasks are mixed together. Methods could have been used to divide the program into smaller parts. However, when I presented this program in Chapter 8, methods had not yet been introduced.

11.1.1 Objects

I will now go beyond methods and treat the crossword puzzle as a new *data type*. First, I will pretend that Java already includes this data type. Later, I will show you how to extend Java with this data type. Here we go.

The statement

```
puzzle p = new puzzle("hangman");
```

defines a variable p, which holds the complete and partial solutions to a crossword puzzle. The complete solution is automatically input from a text file, named hangman. In formal terms, the variable p is said to hold an *object* of a new data type, named puzzle.

A program cannot access the puzzle p directly. However, the following method calls provide *indirect access* to the object or *class instance* p:

- p.solved()

  Returns a `boolean` value. If the `puzzle p` has been solved, the value is `true`; otherwise, it is `false`.

- p.highlight(ch);

  Extends the partial solution of the puzzle p with every occurrence of the character `ch`.

- p.display(out);

  Displays the partial solution of the puzzle p.

Using these methods, I can write a much nicer version of the main loop:

```
{ ...
  puzzle p = new puzzle("hangman");
  ...
  while (!p.solved() & ...)
    { ...
      char ch = in.read();
      p.highlight(ch);
      p.display(out);
      ...
    }
  ...
}
```

11.1.2 Class Definitions

In our daily lives, we often describe objects in terms of what we can *do* with them: a hammer is a tool that can *hit* another object; a chair is an object you can *sit* on. Similarly, you might describe a `puzzle` as an object you can do three things with: you can test if it has been `solved`, `highlight` it, or `display` it. That's all.

From a programmer's point of view, then, a `puzzle` is just a group of related methods. In other words, it is a `class`. Here is an outline of the class, named `puzzle`:

```
class puzzle
{ private char a[][], b[][];
  private int n;

  public puzzle(String data) throws Exception
  { ... }

  public void display(output out) throws Exception
```

```
    { ... }

    public boolean solved()
    { ... }

    public void highlight(char ch)
    { ... }
}
```

This *class definition* consists of a heading and a body. The *class heading*

```
class puzzle
```

defines the *class name* puzzle. The *class body* defines

- Three variables a, b, and n. Since every puzzle object has its own instances of these variables, they are known as the *object variables* of the class.

- An *object constructor*, which initializes the object variables of a particular puzzle object. The constructor has the same name as the class.

- Three *object methods*, which can be used to solve the puzzle.

11.1.3   Object Constructors

The execution of the statement

```
puzzle p = new puzzle("hangman");
```

creates a new puzzle object p in two steps:

1. The object variables a, b, and n are created as new variables associated with the object. (Conceptually, these variable instances exist until the program execution ends.)

2. The constructor body is executed with the actual string parameter "hangman".

The object constructor inputs the solution to the crossword puzzle from a text file and initializes the matrix instances a and b:

```
public puzzle(String data) throws Exception
{ input in = new input(data);
  n = in.readint();
  a = new char[n+1][n+1];
```

```
b = new char[n+1][n+1];
for (int i = 1; i <= n; i++)
  { for (int j = 1; j <= n; j++)
      { in.readblanks();
        char ch = in.read();
        a[i][j] = ch;
        b[i][j] = (ch == '.' ? '.' : '?');
      }
    in.readln();
  }
in.close();
}
```

11.1.4 Object Methods

The `highlight` method scans the complete solution to a particular puzzle. Wherever it finds a given character `ch` it assigns the same character to the corresponding element of the partial solution:

```
public void highlight(char ch)
{ for (int i = 1; i <= n; i++)
    for (int j = 1; j <= n; j++)
      if (a[i][j] == ch) b[i][j] = ch;
}
```

This method is invoked by writing the name of an object, followed by the method name and an actual parameter:

```
p.highlight(ch);
```

The object variable p serves as an *implicit reference parameter*. It *binds* the variable names a, b, and n to the instances of these variables that are associated with the particular object p.

The boolean function `solved` scans the partial solution of a puzzle p and counts all characters except the question marks. If the number of known characters is equal to the total number of characters in the $n \times n$ complete solution, the value of the function call `p.solved()` is `true`; otherwise, it is `false`.

```
public boolean solved()
{ int count = 0;
  for (int i = 1; i <= n; i++)
    for (int j = 1; j <= n; j++)
      if (b[i][j] != '?') count = count + 1;
  return count == n*n;
}
```

The `display` method is straightforward:

```
public void display(output out) throws Exception
{ for (int i = 1; i <= n; i++)
    { for (int j = 1; j <= n; j++)
        out.write(" " + b[i][j]);
      out.writeln();
    }
  out.writeln();
}
```

11.1.5   The Program "Hangman II"

Program 11.1 *Hangman II.*

```
class puzzle
{ private char a[][], b[][];
  private int n;

  public puzzle(String data) throws Exception
  { input in = new input(data);
    n = in.readint();
    a = new char[n+1][n+1];
    b = new char[n+1][n+1];
    for (int i = 1; i <= n; i++)
      { for (int j = 1; j <= n; j++)
          { in.readblanks();
            char ch = in.read();
            a[i][j] = ch;
            b[i][j] = (ch == '.' ? '.' : '?');
          }
        in.readln();
      }
    in.close();
  }

  public void display(output out) throws Exception
  { for (int i = 1; i <= n; i++)
      { for (int j = 1; j <= n; j++)
          out.write(" " + b[i][j]);
        out.writeln();
      }
    out.writeln();
  }

  public boolean solved()
  { int count = 0;
    for (int i = 1; i <= n; i++)
      for (int j = 1; j <= n; j++)
        if (b[i][j] != '?') count = count + 1;
    return count == n*n;
```

```
    }

  public void highlight(char ch)
  { for (int i = 1; i <= n; i++)
      for (int j = 1; j <= n; j++)
        if (a[i][j] == ch) b[i][j] = ch;
  }
}

class hangman extends basic
{ public static void main(String param[]) throws Exception
  { input in = new input();
    output out = new output();
    out.writeln("Type maximum number of guesses");
    int max = in.readint();
    puzzle p = new puzzle("hangman");
    int guesses = 0;
    while (!p.solved() & (guesses < max))
      { out.writeln("Type a letter");
        out.writeln();
        in.readblanks();
        char ch = in.read();
        p.highlight(ch);
        p.display(out);
        guesses = guesses + 1;
      }
    out.writeln("You " + (p.solved() ?" won" : "lost")
      + " after " + guesses + " guesses");
    in.close(); out.close();
  }
}
```

11.1.6 Information Hiding

The keyword public in front of the object methods indicates that these methods may be invoked outside the class by writing, say,

```
p.display(out);
```

However, since the object variables are labeled private, they can only be accessed inside the class. Any attempt to use these variables outside the class, say,

```
p.n = 0;
```

will be reported as an error during compilation:

```
Variable n in class puzzle not accessible
```

The object variables are, in effect, hidden inside the class. This is known as *information hiding.* The advantages of this idea will be discussed later.

11.2   DATA STRUCTURES

I am going to show you how to define a class that records an *invocation trace* during the execution of the *recursive calculator* (Program 10.2). As an example, the evaluation of the expression

```
(2 + 15) - ((1 - 3) + 4)
```

should print a trace that begins as follows (see 10.2.3):

```
expr term expr term return 2
expr term expr
expr term expr ...
...
```

This trace is printed according to the following rules:

- *Rule 1*: At the beginning of a function invocation, the function name is printed on the current line.

- *Rule 2*: At the end of an invocation, the function result is printed on the current line. The remaining previous activations are then listed on the next two lines. (Subsequent invocations may extend the last line until another invocation returns a result.)

Before I attempt to print such a trace, I will solve a simpler problem first.

11.2.1   The Stack Concept

Rule 2 (above) requires the program to keep track of the names of all incomplete invocations. This is easy to do with paper and pencil. When the first invocation begins, write the corresponding function name on a piece of paper, and put it in front of you. At the beginning of the second invocation, write the corresponding function name on another piece of paper, and put it on top of the first piece, and so on. When a function invocation ends, remove the piece of paper at the top of the pile and throw it away. The rest of the pile now shows the names of all previous calls, which are still in progress. When the first invocation ends and the last piece of paper is removed, the pile is empty (as it was to begin with).

So, we need something similar to a pile of paper with the ability to add
and remove pieces of paper at the top of the pile. This type of data structure
is called a *stack*, because it is similar to a stack of plates in a cafeteria. When
you remove a plate from a stack, the one you remove is always the last one
that was placed in the stack. That is why a stack is also known as a *last-in,
first-out memory.*

For the tracing problem, I will again begin by inventing a programming
notation for a stack. The statement

```
stack lifo = new stack(4);
```

creates an *empty* `stack`, named `lifo`, with room for up to four strings. The
following method calls apply to this stack:

- `lifo.more()`

  Returns a `boolean` value, which is `true` only if the `stack lifo` holds
  one or more strings.

- `lifo.push(s);`

  Adds a string `s` on top of the `stack lifo`.

- `lifo.pop()`

  Returns the string at the top of the `stack lifo` and removes it from
  the stack.

The following procedure statements push four function names on the
stack:

```
lifo.push("expr");
lifo.push("term");
lifo.push("expr");
lifo.push("term");
```

At this point, the stack can be pictured as follows:

```
4 | "term" |
3 | "expr" |
2 | "term" |
1 | "expr" |
```

The stack *indices* define the order in which the names were pushed on the
stack. The current *depth* of the stack is 4.

Since invocation traces are printed line by line, it may be more helpful to view the stack as a data structure that grows horizontally, from left to right:

"expr"	"term"	"expr"	"term"
1	2	3	4

It is now easy to see that the stack holds the first four names of the invocation trace. Needless to say, this trace was *not* recorded by the calculator program.

When the fourth invocation terminates, the corresponding function name must be popped from the stack, say,

```
String top = lifo.pop();
```

The stack now holds the function names that should appear on the second line of the invocation trace:

"expr"	"term"	"expr"
1	2	3

11.2.2   The Class Stack

The following **class** defines the data type **stack**:

```
class stack extends basic
{ private String table[];
  private int depth;

  public stack(int maxdepth)
  { table = new String[maxdepth+1];
    depth = 0;
  }

  public boolean more()
  { return depth > 0; }

  public void push(String value)
  { depth = depth + 1;
    table[depth] = value;
  }

  public String pop()
  { String value = table[depth];
    depth = depth - 1;
    return value;
```

```
    }
}
```

The execution of the statement

```
stack lifo = new stack(4);
```

creates a new stack object lifo with two *object variables*:

- The contents of this stack is kept in an array, named table, with room for 4 strings.

- The stack depth is an integer variable initialized to 0.

The procedure call

```
lifo.push("expr");
```

increments the stack depth by one and assigns the string "expr" to the corresponding stack element.

The pop method is very similar.

11.2.3   Testing a Class

A class should be tested using the same guidelines that apply to the testing of any other program component (see 3.2). The testing is done by including the class in a test program that includes a main method written for this purpose.

Program 11.2 is a test program, which ensures that every statement in the class is executed at least once. A class should not be used in any other program until it has passed such a test. The documentation of a class should include the program that was used to test it systematically.

Program 11.2 *Stack Test.*

```
/* Tests the methods of a string stack. */

class stack
{ private String table[];
  private int depth;

  public stack(int maxdepth)
  { table = new String[maxdepth+1];
    depth = 0;
  }
```

```
    public boolean more()
    { return depth > 0; }

    public void push(String value)
    { depth = depth + 1;
      table[depth] = value;
    }

    public String pop()
    { String value = table[depth];
      depth = depth - 1;
      return value;
    }
}

class stacktest extends basic
{ public static void main(String param[]) throws Exception
  { output out = new output("results");
    stack lifo = new stack(4);
    lifo.push("expr"); lifo.push("term");
    lifo.push("expr"); lifo.push("term");
    while (lifo.more())
      out.writeln(lifo.pop());
    out.close();
  }
}
```

11.2.4   Abstract Data Types

In Brinch Hansen (1977), I wrote:

> The combination of a data structure and the operations used to access
> it is called an *abstract data type*. It is abstract because the rest of the
> system only needs to know what operations one can perform on it but
> can ignore the details of how they are carried out.

The classes discussed so far define two abstract data types, named `puzzle`
and `stack`.

The class notation enables a compiler to check that the class methods
are the only operations performed on an abstract data type. This *access
control* prevents the rest of a program from assigning meaningless values to
object variables and making an already tested class fail.

11.3 CLASS HIERARCHIES

A `stack` can only keep track of function names during invocations. We must now decide how an invocation trace should be printed.

11.3.1 Printing an Invocation Trace

Suppose the recursive calculator prints its own invocation trace while it runs. At some point the first line of the trace might list three incomplete function calls in progress:

```
expr term expr
```

When `expression` calls `term` again, the latter function *extends the trace* by adding its own name on the first line:

```
expr term expr term
```

When this invocation is ready to return a value, the function *reduces the trace* in three steps:

1. The function result is added at the end of the first line:

   ```
   expr term expr term result 2
   ```

2. The function name `term` is popped from the stack and a list of the three remaining invocations is printed on the second line:

   ```
   expr term expr term result 2
   expr term expr
   ```

3. The remaining invocations are repeated on the third line (without a newline character):

   ```
   expr term expr term result 2
   expr term expr
   expr term expr
   ```

When the execution continues, the (incomplete) third line may be extended by further invocations until it is terminated by another return.

11.3.2 Trace Methods

I need two methods that can `extend` and `reduce` an invocation trace as described above. These methods will be called at the beginning and end of each calculator function. For example:

```
static int Term(input in) throws Exception
{ extend("term");
  ...
  reduce(value);
  return value;
}
```

The function `expression` will be modified similarly.

Where should the trace methods be defined? One possibility is to put them inside the class `stack` and change its name to, say, `tracestack`:

```
class tracestack
{ private String table[];
  private int depth;
  private output out;

  public tracestack(int maxdepth)
  { ... }

  public boolean more()
  { ... }

  public void push(String value)
  { ...

  public String pop()
  { ... }

  public void extend(String name) throws Exception
  { ... }

  public void reduce(int value) throws Exception
  { ... }
}
```

Although this idea works, it is not very helpful. The `stack` definition should be part of a *library* of classes that can be used in many applications. This simple concept should be left as is and not be complicated by the need for a more specialized `tracestack`.

11.3.3 Hierarchical Classification

The organization of any library is based on the idea of classifying books and periodicals in such a way that related literature can be found in the same place in the library (or its catalog). A classification of computing literature may, for example, include the following categories:

```
D. Software
   D.1  Programming Techniques
        D.1.1  Object-Oriented Programming
```

The literature on *software* includes a subclass on *programming techniques*, which in turn includes another subclass on *object-oriented programming*.

A subclass is more specialized than the general classes listed above it. As an example, *object-oriented programming* refines or *extends* our general understanding of *programming techniques*. The relationship between these categories can also be described as follows:

- The *software* category covers all literature on computer software.

- The *programming techniques* category extends the *software* category.

- The *object-oriented programming* category extends the *programming techniques* category.

This example illustrates another human thinking habit: *we often find it helpful to describe the world as hierarchical structures that include general and specialized variants of related ideas.*

11.3.4 Subclasses

Thinking about programming is no different than thinking about anything else. In object-oriented programming, we need to be able to extend classes with subclasses, which define specialized variants of more general data structures.

The following defines a **class tracestack**, which **extends** the **class stack**:

```
class tracestack extends stack
{ private output out;

  public tracestack(int maxdepth) throws Exception
  { super(maxdepth);
    out = new output("results");
  }

  public void close() throws Exception
  { out.close(); }
```

```
private void display() throws Exception
{ for (int i = 1; i <= depth; i++)
    out.write(table[i] + " ");
}

public void extend(String name) throws Exception
{ push(name); out.write(name + " "); }

public void reduce(int value) throws Exception
{ out.writeln("return " + value);
  String top = pop(); display();
  out.writeln(); display();
}
}
```

The class tracestack is a *subclass* of the class stack. Conversely, the stack is regarded as a *superclass* of the tracestack.

A class and its superclass are equivalent to a single class that combines the variables and methods of both classes. If you open a new tracestack

```
tracestack t = new tracestack(100);
```

it will be associated with fresh instances of the object variables of a tracestack and a simple stack:

```
private String table[];
private int depth;
private output out;
```

For the object t, you can use both tracestack methods and stack methods. For example:

```
t.push(name);
t.extend("term");
```

However, in the same program, you can also declare a simple stack

```
stack s = new stack(20);
```

and apply the stack methods to it. For example:

```
String top = s.pop();
```

Although t and s are *similar objects*, they are nevertheless objects of *different types*. Consequently, you cannot apply a tracestack method, say,

```
s.reduce(value);
```

to a stack s.

11.3.5   The Program "Invocation Trace"

Program 11.3 *Invocation Trace.*

```
/* Outputs an invocation trace of the recursive calculator. */

class stack extends basic
{ protected String table[];
  protected int depth;

  public stack(int maxdepth)
  { table = new String[maxdepth+1];
    depth = 0;
  }

  public boolean more()
  { return depth > 0; }

  public void push(String value)
  { depth = depth + 1;
    table[depth] = value;
  }

  public String pop()
  { String value = table[depth];
    depth = depth - 1;
    return value;
  }
}

class tracestack extends stack
{ private output out;

  public tracestack(int maxdepth) throws Exception
  { super(maxdepth);
    out = new output("results");
  }

  public void close() throws Exception
  { out.close(); }

  private void display() throws Exception
  { for (int i = 1; i <= depth; i++)
      out.write(table[i] + " ");
  }

  public void extend(String name) throws Exception
  { push(name); out.write(name + " "); }

  public void reduce(int value) throws Exception
  { out.writeln("return " + value);
```

```
      String top = pop(); display();
      out.writeln(); display();
    }
}

class calculator extends tracestack
{ private input in;

  public calculator(String data) throws Exception
  { super(100); in = new input(data); }

  private int Term() throws Exception
  { extend("term");
    int value;
    in.readblanks();
    if (in.digit())
      value = in.readint();
    else
      { char ch = in.read();
        assume(ch == '(');
        value = Expression();
        in.readblanks();
        ch = in.read();
        assume(ch == ')');
      }
    in.readblanks();
    reduce(value);
    return value;
  }

  private int Expression() throws Exception
  { extend("expr");
    int value = Term();
    while ((in.next() == '+') | (in.next() == '-'))
      { char ch = in.read();
        if (ch == '+') value = value + Term();
        else value = value - Term();
      }
    reduce(value);
    return value;
  }

  public void Text() throws Exception
  { int value = Expression();
    while (in.more())
      value = Expression();
  }
}

class invocation extends basic
{ public static void main(String param[]) throws Exception
```

```
  { calculator adder = new calculator("expressions");
    adder.Text(); adder.close();
  }
}
```

Comments:

1. Program 11.3 defines a hierarchy of three related classes:

   ```
   class stack extends basic
   class tracestack extends stack
   class calculator extends tracestack
   ```

2. The `stack extends basic` to enable the subclass `calculator` to use the method `assume` defined by the Java text program (see 2.7).

3. The simple idea that a class hierarchy combines the attributes of all its classes requires a minor modification in Java. If a class refers directly to the private variables of one of its superclasses, these variables must be labeled as `protected` (instead of `private`). As an example, the `display` method of a `tracestack` refers to the `table` and `depth` variables of the corresponding `stack`.

4. Apart from the above modification, the `class stack` is left unchanged (even though the program does *not* use the method `more`).

5. The `calculator class` includes an object constructor with the same name as the class. Since a calculator extends a `tracestack`, the particular tracestack used by a calculator has no name. Instead, the calculator constructor uses the notation `super(100)` to invoke the object constructor of its immediate superclass (the `tracestack`).

6. Since the class `calculator extends tracestack`, every calculator is also a tracestack, which includes the `extend` and `reduce` methods. Consequently, a calculator does not need a tracestack variable to invoke these methods.

11.4 THE TRAVELING SALESPERSON

A salesperson must visit each of n cities once and return to the initial city. The aim is to find the shortest possible tour. At least one book is dedicated exclusively to this famous optimization problem (Lawler 1990).

In theory, *The Traveling Salesperson Problem* is easy to solve. Write a computer program that (somehow) generates all the possible ways in which the cities can be listed, one after the other. Let the program compute the length of each tour and choose the shortest one.

Unfortunately, the number of possible tours is astronomical even for a modest number of cities. Suppose a computer can examine 1 million tours per second (Brinch Hansen 1995):

> In that case, you can find a minimum tour of 15 cities in about two weeks. However, a 24-city problem would require 20 billion years, which is about four times the age of Earth (Sagan 1980). So *exhaustive search* is out of the question.
>
> Since it is impractical to consider all possible tours of n cities, I will examine only a *random sample* of tours. The idea is to make random changes of an initial tour in the hope of finding shorter and shorter tours. This statistical approach is an example of the *Monte Carlo* method of computing.

The Monte Carlo method is named after the famous resort town in Monaco that has the world's oldest casino.

The TSP problem belongs to a class of computational problems known as *NP-complete problems*. Although nobody knows for sure, it is believed that no computer will ever be able to solve any of these problems in a reasonable amount of time. For these intractable problems, we must be satisfied with *probabilistic programs* that find *near-optimal solutions*. I will explain a straightforward Monte Carlo method for the TSP problem.

11.4.1   The Manhattan Salesperson

In general, you never know how close an approximate solution is to the (unknown) shortest tour of, say, 16 cities. So, if you write a probabilistic TSP program, you have no idea of how accurate it is!

The best you can do is to experiment with a test case that has a known optimal solution. My test case is a *square grid* of 16 cities:

The cities are separated by horizontal and vertical distances of the same length. Since these distances are the same everywhere, I will measure all distances on the grid in terms of this *unit length*.

The distance between two cities is at least 1 unit. Consequently, a closed tour of 16 cities must at least be 16 units long. The following figure shows that a tour of this length does indeed exist:

The grid is a matrix of cities arranged in four columns and four rows:

```
     1   2   3   4
1    q   •   •   •
2    •   •   •   p
3    •   •   •   •
4    •   •   •   •
```

The location of a city is defined by its column and row numbers. These two numbers are called the x and y *coordinates* of the city.

Examples:

City	x	y
p	4	2
q	1	1

The most direct route from city p to city q is a straight line, which is approximately 3.16 units long. To avoid the use of real numbers, I will assume that the salesperson can only move up, down, left, and right in the grid. All distances can then be represented exactly by integers. This variant of the problem is called the *Manhattan TSP*.

The *Manhattan distance* between two cities is the sum of their horizontal and vertical distances.

Example:

```
distance(p,q) = 3 + 1 = 4
```

11.4.2   Input/Output Format

Before you can write a TSP program, you must choose a data representation of a tour. *The choice of a data representation is a critical programming decision.* If your data structure is convenient for the task at hand, you should be able to write a simple program. However, if a data structure is awkward to use, the only sensible thing to do is to experiment with another one.

Sometimes it is easier to *use different data representations to solve different aspects of the same problem.* For the TSP problem, I found it convenient to use two different data representations of the same tour.

The TSP problem is solved in three phases:

1. *Input* an initial random tour.

2. *Reduce* the tour as much as possible.

3. *Output* the final tour.

During the *input/output phases*, the main concern is to find a data format that is easily comprehended by the user. The following matrix shows an initial *random tour* of the cities:

```
 2 11  9 15
10  3  5  1
16 12  7 13
 8  4  6 14
```

I will call this a *city matrix* or a `map` of the tour.

The numbers show the order in which the cities are visited. The salesperson starts from city number 1 (also known as p) and proceeds to city number 2 (or q). After visiting cities 3, 4, ..., 16, the salesperson returns to city 1. The *Manhattan length* of this tour is 44, which is almost three times longer than the shortest possible tour of length 16.

11.4.3   Data Manipulation

For the *tour reduction*, it is important to use a data structure that makes it easy to change a tour and compute its length. The initial tour is a randomly chosen sequence of the cities. The program randomly selects two cities and exchanges them in the tour. The new tour is accepted if it is shorter than the previous one. Random exchanges of cities are performed thousands of times in the hope that the final tour will be as short as possible.

Instead of using a tour map, imagine that you use paper and pencil to write down a list of the cities in the order in which they will be visited. If each city is written on a separate line, you can use eraser and pencil to exchange two cities on the list.

In a computer, a list of cities can be stored in a simple array. Each element of the array holds the coordinates of a single city. The array indices define the order in which the cities are visited. This data representation of a tour will be called a *city list* or just a `tour`.

Here is an array that holds the *initial random tour* of the 16 cities:

	x	y	
1	4	2	
2	1	1	
3	2	2	
4	2	4	←
5	3	2	
6	3	4	
7	3	3	
8	1	4	
9	3	1	
10	1	2	
11	2	1	
12	2	3	
13	4	3	
14	4	4	←
15	4	1	
16	1	3	

The tour begins at city number 1, which has coordinates (4,2). The final stage of the tour is a trip from city number 16 at (1,3) to city number 1.

This data representation is obviously not very convenient for human comprehension. It is, however, well-suited for data manipulation of a tour:

- The *tour length* is the sum of the distances from city 1 to city 2, from city 2 to city 3, and so on. It includes the final distance from city 16 back to city 1. These distances can be computed from the city coordinates as explained earlier.

- A *tour change* involves selecting two cities at random, say, cities 4 and 14. (In the initial tour list shown above, these cities are marked by arrows.) When these two cities are *exchanged*, you get a slightly different tour:

	x	y	
1	4	2	
2	1	1	
3	2	2	
4	4	4	←
5	3	2	
6	3	4	
7	3	3	
8	1	4	
9	3	1	
10	1	2	
11	2	1	
12	2	3	
13	4	3	
14	2	4	←
15	4	1	
16	1	3	

The corresponding map is shown below:

```
 2 11   9 15
10  3   5  1
16 12   7 13
 8 14   6  4
```

Unfortunately, this tour has a length of 50. Since it is longer than the initial tour, this tour is *rejected*. (The attempted change is undone by exchanging the same two cities again.)

11.4.4 The Greedy Method

The TSP program makes numerous attempts to reduce the tour length by exchanging randomly chosen cities: shorter tours are always accepted; longer ones are always rejected. This approach is known as the *greedy method* of optimization.

Since the TSP program uses random numbers, the tour changes will generally vary from one execution to another. The following results were obtained during a particular execution.

Of the first 10 attempted changes only four were accepted, producing a shorter tour of length 32:

```
 1 11  3  2
10  4  5 15
 9 12  7 13
 8 16  6 14
```

As the tour got shorter, most random changes produced longer tours that were rejected. After 100 attempts, the tour had only been reduced six times, and now had a length of 26:

```
 3  1  2 16
11  4 12 15
 9  5  6 14
10  8 13  7
```

991 of 1000 attempted changes were rejected. The nine accepted changes reduced the tour length to 20:

```
 3  2  1 16
 4 12  5 13
10 11  6 14
 9  8  7 15
```

Finally, after 10000 attempted and 11 accepted changes, I obtained a *shortest tour* of length 16:

```
 3  2  1 16
 4  9 10 15
 5  8 11 14
 6  7 12 13
```

Notice that this is not the same tour as the shortest one shown earlier (see 11.4.1).

It does not matter that 99.89% of the 10000 attempted changes were wasted. In a few seconds the program solved a problem that would have taken many months of computing if each and every tour had to be examined. This is a miraculous outcome of blind luck!

The catch is that I had no way of knowing in advance if the program would ever find a shortest tour and how many attempts it would need to do this. Later, I will show you another example, where the greedy method does not work quite as well.

With this background, I will explain a TSP program that defines cities, tours, and maps by classes.

11.4.5   The City Class

A `city` is represented by its x and y coordinates. Since the rest of the
program will use city coordinates extensively, these object variables are deliberately made `public`.

```
class city
{ public int x, y;

  public city(int i, int j)
  { x = i; y = j; }

  public city copy()
  { return new city(x, y); }

  private static int abs(int value)
  { return value < 0 ? - value : value; }

  public static int distance(city p, city q)
  { return abs(p.x - q.x) + abs(p.y - q.y); }
}
```

The statements

```
city p = new city(4, 2);
city q = new city(1, 1);
```

create two objects p and q that represent cities with coordinates (4,2) and
(1,1), respectively.

The function call

```
p.copy()
```

returns a city object with the same coordinates as the object p.

The function call

```
distance(p, q)
```

returns the integer distance between cities p and q.

The distance from p to q is computed as follows:

```
distance(p,q) = (p.x - q.x) + (p.y - q.y)
             = (4 - 1) + (2 - 1)
             = 3 + 1
             = 4
```

If you use this method to compute the same distance in the opposite
direction, you get a negative value:

```
distance(q,p) = (q.x - p.x) + (q.y - p.y)
             = (1 - 4) + (1 - 2)
             = -3 - 1
             = -4
```

To avoid negative distances, the class uses a private function `abs` that returns the *absolute magnitude* of an integer value independent of its sign. As an example, `abs(-3)` and `abs(3)` are both equal to 3.

11.4.6 Object and Class Methods

The `class city` defines three different kinds of methods:

- An *object constructor* has direct access to the variables of a new object:

  ```
  public city(int i, int j)
  { x = i; y = j; }
  ```

  A call of this constructor includes an *implicit* object parameter p:

  ```
  city p = new city(4, 2);
  ```

- An *object method* has direct access to the variables of an existing object:

  ```
  public city copy()
  { return new city(x, y); }
  ```

  A call of this method also includes an *implicit* object parameter p:

  ```
  p.copy();
  ```

- A *class method* does not have direct access to object variables. The definition of a class method includes the keyword `static`:

  ```
  public static int distance(city p, city q)
  { return abs(p.x - q.x) + abs(p.y - q.y); }
  ```

  A call of this method includes *explicit* object parameters p and q:

  ```
  distance(p, q)
  ```

11.4.7   The Map Class

A map is represented by a matrix that holds s×s integers:

```
class map
{ protected int[][] grid;
  protected int s;

  public map(input in) throws Exception
  { s = in.readint();
    grid = new int[s+1][s+1];
    for (int i = 1; i <= s; i++)
      for (int j = 1; j <= s; j++)
        grid[i][j] = in.readint();
  }

  public void newmap(city[] route, int n)
  { for (int k = 1; k <= s*s; k++)
      { int i = route[k].x;
        int j = route[k].y;
        grid[i][j] = k;
      }
  }

  public void write(output out) throws Exception
  { for (int i = 1; i <= s; i++)
      { for (int j = 1; j <= s; j++)
          out.write(grid[i][j], 3);
        out.writeln();
      }
    out.writeln();
  }
}
```

The statement

```
map m = new map(in);
```

creates a map m. The linear dimension s and the map elements are input from an open text file, named in.

Since the program uses two different data representations of the same tour, it must be able to convert a city list into the corresponding city matrix (and vice versa). The procedure call

```
m.newmap(route);
```

makes the map m describe the same tour as a city list, named route.

The procedure call

```
m.write(out);
```

outputs the map m to an open text file, named out.

11.4.8 The Tour Class

The class tour is a subclass of the class map. A tour of n cities is represented by a city list, named route:

```
class tour extends map
{ private city[] route;
  private int n;

  public tour(input in) throws Exception
  { super(in); n = s*s;
    route = new city[n+1];
    for (int i = 1; i <= s; i++)
      for (int j = 1; j <= s; j++)
        { int k = grid[i][j];
          route[k] = new city(i,j);
        }
  }

  private void exchange(int i, int j)
  { city ri = route[i].copy();
    city rj = route[j].copy();
    route[i] = rj;
    route[j] = ri;
  }

  public int length()
  { int sum =
      city.distance(route[n], route[1]);
    for (int k = 1; k <= n - 1; k++)
      sum = sum +
        city.distance(route[k], route[k+1]);
    return sum;
  }

  public void shorten() throws Exception
  { random chance = new random(1, n);
    int min = length();
    for (int k = 1; k <= 1000*n; k++)
      { int i = chance.readint();
        int j = chance.readint();
        exchange(i, j);
        int next = length();
        if (next <= min) min = next;
        else exchange(i, j);
      }
    newmap(route, n);
  }

  public void write(output out) throws Exception
  { super.write(out);
    out.writeln("length " + length());
    out.writeln();
  }
}
```

The statement

```
tour a = new tour(in);
```

creates an object a that inputs an initial tour from an open text file.

The tour constructor invokes the constructor of its superclass, the map class, which then inputs the initial city matrix. The tour constructor uses this matrix to create the corresponding city list.

The procedure call

```
a.shorten();
```

uses a random number generator to exchange two cities at a time in the city list. If a change does not increase the tour length, it is accepted; otherwise, it is rejected (by exchanging the same cities again). After a fixed number of attempted changes, the final city list is used to compute the corresponding newmap.

Notice that a new tour is accepted even if it is of the same length as the previous one. Although such changes appear to be superfluous, they tend to make the final tour shorter than it would otherwise be. I am not quite sure why this makes a difference, but it does.

The map and tour classes both include a write procedure. The tour procedure uses the statement super.write(out) to call the corresponding map procedure.

11.4.9   Program Documentation

In Chapter 3, I emphasized that

- *Programs should be easy to read, but not necessarily easy to write!*

Believe me, it was not a trivial task for me to write the TSP program. I wrote an earlier version that worked fine. However, since it was slightly awkward to describe, I rewrote the program completely using a different terminology. To make it *readable*, I carefully divided the program into smaller parts, which can be explained separately. The final program consists of three classes. Each class defines only a handful of methods and can be printed on a single page (or less). No method exceeds a dozen lines of program text.

It may surprise you that I wrote ten pages to describe a two-page program. This has been true throughout my career (Brinch Hansen 1996):

I have always found that a good *description* of a program is considerably longer than the program text. Fifteen years ago, I put it this way: "Programming is the art of writing essays in crystal clear prose and making them executable" (Brinch Hansen 1977).

Besides *intellect*, the most valuable asset of a programmer is her ability to *write clearly*.

11.4.10 The Program "The Traveling Salesperson"

Program 11.4 *The Traveling Salesperson.*

```
/* Uses the greedy method and Manhattan
   distances to find a short tour through
   a square grid of n = s*s cities.
*/

class city
{ public int x, y;

  public city(int i, int j)
  { x = i; y = j; }

  public city copy()
  { return new city(x, y); }

  private static int abs(int value)
  { return value < 0 ? - value : value; }

  public static int distance(city p, city q)
  { return abs(p.x - q.x) + abs(p.y - q.y); }
}

class map
{ protected int[][] grid;
  protected int s;

  public map(input in) throws Exception
  { s = in.readint();
    grid = new int[s+1][s+1];
    for (int i = 1; i <= s; i++)
      for (int j = 1; j <= s; j++)
        grid[i][j] = in.readint();
  }

  public void newmap(city[] route, int n)
  { for (int k = 1; k <= s*s; k++)
      { int i = route[k].x;
        int j = route[k].y;
```

```
            grid[i][j] = k;
        }
    }

    public void write(output out) throws Exception
    { for (int i = 1; i <= s; i++)
        { for (int j = 1; j <= s; j++)
            out.write(grid[i][j], 3);
          out.writeln();
        }
      out.writeln();
    }
}

class tour extends map
{ private city[] route;
  private int n;

  public tour(input in) throws Exception
  { super(in); n = s*s;
    route = new city[n+1];
    for (int i = 1; i <= s; i++)
      for (int j = 1; j <= s; j++)
        { int k = grid[i][j];
          route[k] = new city(i,j);
        }
  }

  private void exchange(int i, int j)
  { city ri = route[i].copy();
    city rj = route[j].copy();
    route[i] = rj;
    route[j] = ri;
  }

  public int length()
  { int sum =
      city.distance(route[n], route[1]);
    for (int k = 1; k <= n - 1; k++)
      sum = sum +
        city.distance(route[k], route[k+1]);
    return sum;
  }

  public void shorten() throws Exception
  { random chance = new random(1, n);
    int min = length();
    for (int k = 1; k <= 1000*n; k++)
      { int i = chance.readint();
        int j = chance.readint();
        exchange(i, j);
```

```
        int next = length();
        if (next <= min) min = next;
        else exchange(i, j);
      }
    newmap(route, n);
  }

  public void write(output out) throws Exception
  { super.write(out);
    out.writeln("length " + length());
    out.writeln();
  }
}

class salesperson extends basic
{ public static void main(String param[]) throws Exception
  { input in = new input("salesperson");
    output out = new output("results");
    tour a = new tour(in);
    a.write(out); a.shorten();
    a.write(out);
    in.close(); out.close();
  }
}
```

11.4.11   Further Improvements

I used a variant of the TSP program to generate a *random initial tour* of *64 cities* (see Exercise 11.4):

```
42 20 57 10 58  7  9 51
62 50 52  1 61  6 32 29
43 31 47 46 63 54  2 38
48 25 30 14 17  4 53 13
36 19 27 15 35 23 64 24
 8 49 59  3 34 45 22 21
33 40 12 37 44 18 60  5
41 28 56 55 16 26 11 39
```

In one case, Program 11.4 reduced the length of this tour from 328 to 80:

```
25 24 23 59 22 21  9  8
26 62 61 60 58 11 10  7
27 63 64  1 12  2  5  6
28 46 47 14 13  3  4 57
29 45 48 15 16 17 20 56
30 44 49 50 51 18 19 55
31 43 42 41 40 52 53 54
32 33 34 35 36 39 37 38
```

Although the tour length was reduced by a factor of 4, it was still 25% longer than the shortest possible tour of length 64.

The problem is that the *greedy method* is somewhat naive. Imagine a hiker who tries to reach the highest point in a hilly area by always walking uphill (but never downhill). When the hiker is unable to go any higher, she has indeed reached the top of a hill, but there may be taller hills, which can only be reached by temporarily going downhill into a valley.

There is no guarantee that the greedy method will get you close to the shortest possible tour of a large number of cities. In many cases, it may be trapped in a *local minimum* (instead of an *absolute minimum*).

To reduce the odds of being trapped, I let the TSP program accept longer tours of 64 cities with a probability of only 1 in 10000 (see Exercise 11.5). This produced a shorter tour of length 74:

```
52 53 54 56 57 22 25 21
51 50 55 59 58 23 24 20
46 49 45 44 43 27 26 19
47 48 61 60 42 28 17 18
32 31 62 30 41 29 16 15
33 64 63 38 39 40 13 14
34  1  2 37  6  7 12 11
35 36  3  4  5  8  9 10
```

A more refined version of this optimization method is known as *simulated annealing*. This method initially accepts longer tours with high probability. However, as the computation progresses, longer tours are accepted less and less often. Using simulated annealing on a parallel computer programmed in the language *occam*, I found a minimal tour of 100 cities. For 2500 cities, the average tour was only 4% longer than the shortest possible one (Brinch Hansen 1995).

11.5   FINAL REMARKS

Classes and methods support a programming style in which programs are divided into smaller modules that can be studied separately. In an essay on *design principles*, I wrote the following remarks (Brinch Hansen 1996):

> We will be writing ... programs which are so large that one cannot understand them all at once. So we must reason about them in smaller *pieces*. What properties should these pieces have? Well, they should be so small that any one of them is trivial to understand in itself. It would be ideal if they were no more than *one page* of text each so that they can be comprehended at a glance.

...

Program pieces will be built to perform well-defined, simple functions. We will then combine program pieces into larger *configurations* to carry out more complicated functions. This design method is effective because it splits a complicated task into simpler ones: First you convince yourself that the pieces work individually, and then you think about how they work together. During the second part of the argument it is essential to be able to forget how a piece works in detail—otherwise, the problem becomes too complicated.

...

The idea of reasoning first about *what* a piece does and then studying *how* it does it in detail is most effective if we can repeat this process by explaining each piece in terms of simpler pieces which themselves are built from still simpler pieces. So we shall confine ourselves to *hierarchical structures* composed of ... program pieces.

11.6   JAVA PITFALLS

The programming restrictions recommended for strings (2.8), array variables (7.3), and array parameters (9.10) also apply to *objects*:

- **Do not use the assignment operator for objects.**

- **Do not use comparison operators for objects.**

- **Do not return object parameters.**

If you follow these simple precepts, you can ignore the complicated and error-prone concept of *object references* (which I will only mention in passing).

References are data values which conceptually *"point"* to objects. They are used to *link objects* together into data structures known as *lists*, *trees*, and *graphs*. This can only be done if you ignore the recommended programming restrictions. However, before you do that, you need to fully understand the implications and severe pitfalls of using references in Java programs.

In this book, I have also ignored other complicated aspects of Java and its class concept. If you want to know about the missing details, I recommend the book by David Flanagan (1996).

11.7   PROGRAMMING EXERCISES

Exercise 11.1   Submarine Hunt II

Write a Java program that simulates a *Submarine Hunt* (see Exercise 8.3). Your program must include a `class radar`, with two public variables, a public constructor, and a public procedure:

```
public static final int n = 5
```

The dimension of the n×n radar image.

```
public boolean hit
```

Determines whether or not the submarine has been hit.

```
public radar(output out) throws Exception
```

Initializes and displays a blank radar image. Selects a random position of the hidden submarine.

```
public void drop(output out, int i, int j) throws Exception
```

Drops a depth charge in row i and column j, and displays a new radar image showing all misses and a hit (if any).

Your program must also include a `class target`, with two public variables, and two public procedures (but no constructor):

```
public int i, j;
```

The row and column number of the spot in which a depth charge has been (or will be) dropped.

```
public void select(input in, output out, int n) throws Exception
```

Asks the user to type two integers from 1 to n and assigns these values to i and j.

```
public void summarize(output out, int dropped, boolean hit) throws Exception
```

Shows the number of depth charges dropped and whether or not the submarine was hit.

Exercise 11.2   Music

Write a Java program that reads the following list of 15 CDs from an input file:

```
Cannonball Adderly, Somethin' Else, 1958.
Clifford Brown, Clifford Brown Memorial Album, 1953.
Ray Brown, 3 Dimensions, 1991.
Ornette Coleman, The Shape Of Jazz To Come, 1959.
Miles Davis, Birth Of The Cool, 1949.
Bill Evans, Sunday At The Village Vanguard, 1961.
Ella Fitzgerald, Ella and Oscar, 1975.
```

```
Woody Herman, Keeper Of The Flame, 1949.
Earl Hines, Tour De Force, 1972.
Roger Kellaway, Live At Maybeck Recital Hall Vol. 11, 1991.
Gerry Mulligan, In Paris Vol. 1, 1954.
Oscar Peterson, At Zardi's, 1955.
Sonny Rollins, Sonny Rollins Plus 4, 1956.
Bessie Smith, The Collection, 1923.
Art Tatum, Solo Masterpieces Vol. 4, 1953.
```

The program must include a `class album` that keeps the information about a single CD. The private variables of this class define the name of the artist, the title of the album, and the year it was recorded. The class includes a public constructor, a public function, and a public procedure:

```
public album(input in) throws Exception
```

Inputs the information about a single CD.

```
public boolean recorded(int year1, int year2)
```

The value is `true` if the CD was recorded between two given years; otherwise, the value is `false`.

```
public void write(output out) throws Exception
```

Outputs the information about the CD.

Your program must also include a `class collection`, that keeps information about all the CDs in a private array of albums. This class includes a public constructor and two public procedures:

```
public collection(input in) throws Exception
```

Inputs the information about all the CDs.

```
public void sample(output out, int number) throws Exception
```

Outputs the information about a given number of CDs chosen at random.

```
public void subset(output out, int year1, int year2) throws Exception
```

Outputs the information about every CD recorded between two given years.

Use these procedures to output a list of all CDs recorded in the 1950s, and another list of three CDs chosen at random.

Exercise 11.3 Word Translation

Write a Java program that translates simple Danish sentences, word by word, into (fair to poor) English. The program inputs a (tiny) Danish–English dictionary from a textfile, named `dictionary`. Each dictionary entry consists of a Danish word and a corresponding English word. The program inputs Danish sentences from another textfile, named `danish`. Each sentence consists of a single line of lower-case words without punctuation marks. The output of the program consists of the dictionary followed by a word-by-word translation of each sentence. The program must include a class, named `dictionary`, with the following public procedures:

```
public void read(input in) throws Exception
```

Reads the dictionary from an open input file.

```
public void write(output out) throws Exception
```

Writes the dictionary to an open output file.

```
public String translation(String word) throws Exception
```

Returns an English word (if any) corresponding to a given Danish word. (If the word is not in the dictionary, an error message is returned.)

Test the program with the following input text files, which consist of 21 dictionary entries and 6 Danish sentences:

Dictionary Entries:

```
aendrede changed
bog book
det it
doeden death
du you
en a
er is
fjollet silly
gaar goes
haard hard
han he
hans his
hund dog
hvor how
hvordan how
liv life
maa must
om about
selv self
som like
taler speak
```

Danish Sentences:

```
du taler som en bog
doeden aendrede hans liv
hvordan gaar det
han er en haard hund
det maa du selv om
hvor er det fjollet
```

Exercise 11.4 Random Tour

Write a variant of Program 11.4 that generates a random initial tour of a 64-city grid. Starting with a non-random tour, the program (1) performs 64000 random city exchanges, and (2) outputs the final random tour as a city matrix, which can be input and processed by Program 11.4.

Exercise 11.5 The Traveling Salesperson II

Write a variant of Program 11.4 that occasionally accepts longer tours of a 64-city grid. Try different ways of doing this and vary the frequency of these increases until you get as close as possible to a shortest tour of length 64.

Appendix A

JAVA TEXT PROGRAM

I have written a Java program, called the *text program*, that enables you to use text files in your own Java programs. This appendix explains how you install the text program in your own Unix (or Macintosh) directory. It also summarizes what the text program does.

A.1 INSTALLING THE TEXT PROGRAM

At the beginning of the semester your instructor should send you the text program by E-mail. Please follow the steps explained below to install this program:

1. Create a new directory named, say, `myjava`, for all your Java programs. This is *your Java directory*.

2. Move the E-mail message to your Java directory and save it as a text file, named `text.java`.

3. Edit the text file by deleting everything above the line, marked

   ```
   /******** THE FIRST LINE OF THE JAVA TEXT PROGRAM *********/
   ```

   and everything below the line, marked

   ```
   /********* THE LAST LINE OF THE JAVA TEXT PROGRAM *********/
   ```

4. Compile the text program into executable Java code by typing the command

   ```
   javac -nowarn text.java
   ```

5. List your Java directory again and check that the compilation has added 11 code files:

```
basic.class     infile.class    input.class     keyboard.class
outfile.class   output.class    random.class    reader.class
screen.class    test.class      writer.class
```

6. Run a simple test of the text program by typing the command

```
java test
```

If the compilation was successful, you will be asked to type your name. When you have typed your name, say, `Jane Doe`, the program responds with the message: `Welcome to Java, Jane Doe!`

This completes your installation of the text program. Please leave the edited file `text.java` and the compiled `class` files in your Java directory for the rest of the semester. (If you delete a class file by mistake, you must compile the text program again by repeating steps 4–6 above.)*

Note: Your own Java programs will only work if they are included in your Java directory (which also includes the compiled text program).

A.2   THE BASIC CLASS

The `basic` class defines common constants and methods used by most text classes and user programs.

A.2.1   Basic Constants

```
public static final char cr = '\r',  eof = '\uFFFF',
  nl = '\n', sp = ' ';
public static final boolean echo = true;
```

The character constants are named `cr` (carriage return), `eof` (end of file), `nl` (newline), and `sp` (space). The characters `cr`, `nl`, and `sp` are called *blanks*.

The output to a disk file is *echoed* on the screen.

The default directory for disk files, called the *home directory*, is defined by a string constant not shown here. On a *Unix* system, it is the current directory. On a *Macintosh*, the home directory is user-dependent.

---

*To compile the Java text program on a *Macintosh* system, use the mouse to drag the `text.java` icon and drop it on top of the `Java Compiler` icon. To run the program test, drop the `test.class` icon on top of the `Java Runner` icon.

A.2.2 Basic Methods

```
public static void halt(String error) throws Exception
public static void assume(boolean condition, String error)
  throws Exception
public static void assume(boolean condition) throws Exception
```

The statement halt(e) stops program execution with the error message e.[†]

The statement assume(b,e) has no effect if the boolean expression b is true; otherwise, program execution stops with the error message e. The abbreviated form assume(b) displays the standard message invalid assumption.

A.3   THE OUTPUT CLASS

The output class is used to output a text file to a screen or disk. Conceptually, a hidden *file pointer* defines the position of the *next output character* within the file. An output constructor opens an empty file for output and positions the file pointer at the beginning of the file. Each write method outputs one or more characters to the file and moves the file pointer ahead to the next (empty) character position.

A.3.1   Output Constructors

```
public output() throws Exception
public output(String name) throws Exception
public output(String directory, String name) throws Exception
```

The statement

```
output f = new output()
```

opens a screen as an output file f.

The statement

```
output f = new output(n)
```

opens a new disk file, named n, as an output file f. The name n defines a path to the file starting from the home directory.

The statement

```
output f = new output(d,n)
```

opens a new disk file, named n, as an output file f. The file is included in a directory named d. The name d defines a system-dependent path to the directory.

[†] *Note:* This appendix omits the required semicolon at the end of every input/output statement (see 1.2.1).

A.3.2   Output Methods

```
public void write(char value, int width) throws Exception
public void write(char value) throws Exception
public void write(String value, int width) throws Exception
public void write(String value) throws Exception
public void write(boolean value, int width) throws Exception
public void write(boolean value) throws Exception
public void write(int value, int width) throws Exception
public void write(int value) throws Exception
public void write(double value, int width) throws Exception
public void write(double value) throws Exception
public void writeln() throws Exception
public void writeln(boolean value, int width) throws Exception
public void writeln(boolean value) throws Exception
public void writeln(char value, int width) throws Exception
public void writeln(char value) throws Exception
public void writeln(int value, int width) throws Exception
public void writeln(int value) throws Exception
public void writeln(double value, int width) throws Exception
public void writeln(double value) throws Exception
public void writeln(String value, int width) throws Exception
public void writeln(String value) throws Exception
public void writesame(char value, int number) throws Exception
public void writespace(int number) throws Exception
public void close() throws Exception
```

This section defines actions on an output file f:

The statement f.write(e,w) outputs the value of an expression e as a text field of width w. A character or string value is output with trailing spaces (if necessary). A boolean, integer, or double value is output with leading spaces (if necessary).

The statement f.write(e) outputs a character, string, boolean, integer, or double value (without leading or trailing blanks).

The statement f.writeln() outputs an nl character.

The statement f.writeln(e,w) outputs the value of an expression e as a text field of width w, followed by an nl character. A character or string value is output with trailing spaces (if necessary). A boolean, integer, or double value is output with leading spaces (if necessary).

The statement f.writeln(e) outputs a character, string, boolean, integer, or double value e (without leading or trailing blanks), followed by an nl character.

The statement f.writesame(c,n) outputs the same character c, n times.

The statement f.writespace(n) outputs n spaces.

The statement f.close() outputs an eof character and closes the text file for further output.

A.4 THE INPUT CLASS

The `input` class is used to input a text file from a keyboard or disk. Conceptually, a hidden *file pointer* defines the position of the *next input character* within the file. An `input` constructor opens a file for input and positions the file pointer at the beginning of the file. Each `read` method inputs one or more characters from the file and moves the file pointer ahead to the next input character. It is, however, possible to obtain (or classify) the `next` input character without advancing the file pointer. Conversely, the file pointer can also be moved one character ahead (without returning a character).

A.4.1 Input Constructors

```
public input() throws Exception
public input(String name) throws Exception
public input(String directory, String name) throws Exception
```

The statement

```
input f = new input()
```

opens a keyboard as an input file `f`. Keyboard input alternates between two phases: first, the user types and edits a complete line (including a return); then the program inputs the line (including a `nl` character), one character at a time. A typed line consisting of the string `eof` (followed by return) is input as an `eof` character.

The statement

```
input f = new input(n)
```

opens an existing disk file, named `n`, as an input file `f`. The name `n` defines a path to the file starting from the home directory.

The statement

```
input f = new input(d,n)
```

opens an existing disk file, named `n`, as an input file `f`. The file is looked up in a directory named `d`. The name `d` defines a system-dependent path to the directory.

A.4.2 Input Methods

```
public boolean more() throws Exception
public boolean blank() throws Exception
public boolean digit() throws Exception
public boolean letter() throws Exception
public char read() throws Exception
public boolean readboolean() throws Exception
public int readint() throws Exception
public double readdouble() throws Exception
```

```
public String readname() throws Exception
public String readword() throws Exception
public String readline() throws Exception
public void readln() throws Exception
public void readblanks() throws Exception
public char next() throws Exception
public void readnext() throws Exception
public void close() throws Exception
```

This section defines actions on an input file `f`:

The boolean expression `f.more()` is `true` if the next input character is *not* an eof character; otherwise, it is `false`.

The boolean expression `f.blank()` determines whether or not the next input character is a blank.

The boolean expression `f.digit()` determines whether or not the next input character is a digit.

The boolean expression `f.letter()` determines whether or not the next input character is a letter.

The expression `f.read()` inputs a character.

The expression `f.readboolean()` inputs a boolean value (after skipping leading blanks).

The expression `f.readint()` inputs an integer (after skipping leading blanks).

The expression `f.readdouble()` inputs a double value (after skipping leading blanks).

The expression `f.readname()` inputs a string of letters, digits, and underscores (after skipping leading blanks).

The expression `f.readword()` inputs a string of nonblank characters (after skipping leading blanks).

The expression `f.readline()` inputs the rest of a line (including the `nl` character) and returns it as a string (without the `nl` character).

The statement `f.readln()` inputs and skips the rest of a line (including the `nl` character).

The statement `f.readblanks()` inputs and skips a string of blanks (if any).

The expression `f.next()` returns the next input character (without advancing the file pointer).

The statement `f.readnext()` moves the file pointer one character ahead (without returning a character).

The statement `f.close()` closes the text file for further input.

A.5   THE RANDOM CLASS

The `random` class is used to generate random numbers. A `random` constructor opens a generator for input of an unbounded sequence of random numbers. These numbers are uniformly distributed in a given range. A `read` method inputs a random number from the generator.

A.5.1 Random Constructor

```
public random(int min, int max)
```

The statement

```
random r = new random(m,n)
```

opens a new generator r for random numbers with a minimum value m and a maximum value n (provided $m \leq n$). If $m > n$, program execution stops with the error message: `invalid random bounds`.

A.5.2 Random Methods

```
public int readint()
public double readdouble()
public void close()
```

This section defines actions on a random number generator r:

The expression `r.readint()` inputs a random integer in the range

$$m \leq \text{r.readint()} \leq n$$

The expression `r.readdouble()` inputs a random double in the range

$$\text{(double)}m \leq \text{r.readdouble()} \leq \text{(double)}n$$

The statement `r.close()` closes the random number generator for further input.

Appendix B

SAMPLE CLASS SCHEDULE

CLASS	CHAPTER	LECTURE	HOMEWORK	DUE
1	1	Overview. Programs. Output.		
2		Variables. Expressions. Input.		
3	2	Simple choice.		
4	3	Multiple choice.	Exercise 3.2	•7
5		Random choice.		
6	4	Simple repetition.		
• 7	5	Unbounded repetition.	Exercise 5.2	• 11
8		Unbounded repetition.		
9	6	Text files.		
10		Text files.		
• 11	7	Simple arrays.	Exercise 7.2	• 15
12		Simple arrays.		
13	8	Matrices.		
14		Matrices.		
• 15	9	Simple methods.	Exercise 8.3	• 19
16		Parsing methods.		
17		Array parameters.		
18		Array functions.		
• 19		Java Pitfalls.	Exercise 9.4	• 23
20	10	Recursive methods.		
21		Mutual recursion.		
22	11	Class concept.		
• 23		Data structures	Exercise 11.3	• 27
24		Class hierarchies.		
25		The Traveling Salesperson.		
26		The Traveling Salesperson.		
• 27		The Traveling Salesperson.		

REFERENCES

In some cases, this book does not mention the original publications of ideas. Instead, it cites other works by the same authors, which may be more accessible to undergraduates from different academic disciplines.

Asimov, I. 1976. *Science, Numbers, and I.* Ace Books, New York.

Barasch, S., et al., 1991. *GED High School Equivalency Test Examination.* Prentice Hall, New York, 31.

Bell, E. T. 1965. *Men of Mathematics.* Simon & Schuster, New York.

Brinch Hansen, P. 1973. *Operating System Principles.* Prentice Hall, Englewood Cliffs, NJ.

Brinch Hansen, P. 1977. *The Architecture of Concurrent Programs.* Prentice Hall, Englewood Cliffs, NJ.

Brinch Hansen, P. 1985. *Brinch Hansen on Pascal Compilers.* Prentice Hall, Englewood Cliffs, NJ.

Brinch Hansen, P. 1990. The linear search rediscovered. *Structured Programming 11*, 1 (January), 53–55.

Brinch Hansen, P. 1995. *Studies in Computational Science: Parallel Programming Paradigms.* Prentice Hall, Englewood Cliffs.

Brinch Hansen, P. 1996. *The Search for Simplicity: Essays in Parallel Programming.* IEEE Computer Society Press, Los Alamitos, CA.

Cook, R., and Morton, B. 1994. *The Penguin Guide to Jazz on CD, LP and Casette.* Penguin Books, New York.

Dijkstra, E. W. 1982. *Selected Writings on Computing: A Personal Perspective.* Springer-Verlag, New York.

Federal Highway Administration, 1980. *Cost of Owning and Operating Automobiles and Vans.*

Flanagan, D. 1996. *Java in a Nutshell.* O'Reilly & Associates, Cambridge, England.

Flesch, R. 1962. *The Art of Plain Talk.* Collier Books, New York.

Good Time Crossword Puzzles, 1997. Crossword 1. *Good Time Crossword Puzzles, No. 126*, (March).

Gosling, J., Joy, B., and Steele, G. 1996. *The Java Language Specification.* Addison-Wesley, Reading, MA.

Hacker, A., Ed. 1983. *U/S—A Statistical Portrait of the American People.* The Viking Press, New York.

Lawler, E. L., Lenstra, J. K., Rinnooy Kan, A. H. G., and Shmoys, D. B. 1990. *The Traveling Salesman Problem: A Guided Tour of Combinatorial Optimization.* John Wiley & Sons, New York.

Naur, P. 1992. *Computing: A Human Activity.* ACM Press, New York.

Sagan, C. 1980. *Cosmos.* Random House, New York.

Sedgewick, R. 1983. *Algorithms.* Addison-Wesley, Reading, MA.

Strunk, W., and White, E. B. 1959. *The Elements of Style.* Macmillan, New York.

Weaver, W. 1963. *Lady Luck: The Theory of Probability.* Doubleday, Garden City, NY.

Wechsler, J., Ed. 1978. *On Aesthetics in Science.* The MIT Press, Cambridge, MA.

INDEX